# MY REASON.
# MY HERO.

Inspirational True Stories from Successful
Entrepreneurs and Their Amazing Kids

# MY REASON.
# MY HERO.

Inspirational True Stories from Successful
Entrepreneurs and Their Amazing Kids

**Ainsley&Allen**
PUBLISHING

Ainsley & Allen Publishing LLC
2035 Sunset Lake Road
Newark, DE 19702

www.ainsleyallenpublishing.com

My Reason. My Hero.—1st ed.
978-1-946694-17-1

Library of Congress Control Number:  2017958761

# Authors

Brian Ainsley Horn and Bella Horn

Carmen Sakurai and Joshua Sakurai-Maranon

Ryan Stewman and Jax Stewman

Jody Jelas and Milly & Joey Tolhopf

Victor Bell Jr and Aaron Holland Bell

Nora Sudduth and Ryann Sudduth

Kolby Kolibas and Noah Kolibas & Sophie Kolibas

Sara Flowers and Cole Flowers

Mark Evans DM and Mark Evans III

Renée Jean and Leana Marie

Raul Villacis and Alejandro Villacis

Brandon James Duncan and Isla Jo Duncan

Maria Whalen and Riana Whalen

Marshall Sylver and Sterling Sylver

Sarie Taylor and Maia Taylor

Chad Michael Hensley and Gabriel Alexander Hensley

Troy A. Broussard and Thales G. Broussard

Nancy E. Klensch and Griffin Heckford

Jason & Nandi Moore and Bodhi Shonin Moore

Dr. Matt Motil & Grayson, Logan, Peighton, Ella, and Jaxson Motil

James M. Troth and Kaitlyn A. Troth

Andy Hussong and Kurtis Hussong

# Table of Contents

# Introduction

Being a parent, like running a company, can be tough at times. However, being an entrepreneur can put you at an advantage. Entrepreneurs are clever, imaginative and mentally inquisitive by nature, and sharing these unique traits with your kids can help them be successful.

Since the cost of starting a business is dropping, it's likely the next generation will be even more entrepreneurial. So, ingraining these values in your kids now will only benefit them.

Because you are an entrepreneur, the type of discussions and lessons you teach your kids will normally be not the same as those other professions. Your children will naturally ingest your entrepreneurial ethos just by seeing how you live and function.

However, if you want to drive home the most important lessons you've learned along your entrepreneurial journey, you need a plan.

This book is about the lessons that we as entrepreneurs have learned from our kids and applied in our businesses, and about the entrepreneurial lessons our kids have already learned from us.

These are the important lessons that 22 successful entrepreneurs wanted to share with other entrepreneurial parents like you.

Passing on your entrepreneurial values to your kids will give them advantages in life. They'll become strong, confident, independent children and young adults. And because of their independence, you'll be able to focus more on your own business. Sharing these traits will ensure a lasting parent-child relationship.

Enjoy all these stories, and feel free to reach out to any author if you have comments or questions for them.

# Put the Phone Away, Daddy

## Dad's Story

My first child, Jackson, has Down syndrome. He'll need to be taken care of, in some capacity, for the rest of his life.

I know that more than likely I won't be around his whole life. That will leave his care in the hands of his younger sister, Bella, after I'm gone.

I want to make sure that not only is he set up financially, but also that Bella has a lifestyle that will allow them to spend time together as much as they want.

She already displays entrepreneurial traits, so that is a natural path for her.

So, I want to be a good example for her.

Sometimes I am, and sometimes I'm not.

I'm always working or thinking about work – like many other entrepreneurs and passionate professionals.

I'm always closing deals over Facebook Messenger, checking stats on our funnels, or doing research for a new project.

It's hard to turn that passion off when it's part of your DNA.

Of course, I've heard many times that you need to put your phone away when you spend time with your kids – which I thought I did.

I put it away at the park, when we play games, swim, eat dinner, etc.

But one evening while I was making dinner for the kids, I was chatting with my partner on Slack. Bella asked me a simple question, "Daddy, what day is tomorrow?"

It was a simple question, so I didn't even look up from the phone and answered, "Friday."

A few seconds later I felt a little hand on my leg, looked down and saw my angel's face looking up at me with a very serious expression.

"It's not Chuck E Cheese day, Daddy? Aren't you taking me there for lunch?"

I said, "Oh, yes, I'm sorry baby. Tomorrow is Chuck E. Cheese day too. I'll sneak you out of school for our lunch date."

What she said next hit home, "Daddy, you should put the phone away, and look at me. That way you won't be wrong next time."

Now, every single time we talk, I put away the phone, get down on one knee, look at her right in the eye.

If I am on the phone, cooking, or unable to give her my full attention right then, I tell her to wait. As soon as I can get to a stopping point, I do. Then, I get down on one knee and look her in the eye.

Focusing 100% on listening to her in this exact way has been amazing. Even the smallest conversations are bonding... and we have many of them every single day. The connection of being right at her level, looking her directly in the eyes and nodding my head is amazing.

She gets sparkly eyes and a huge smile even when I just answer the simplest question.

## The Lesson

As I've gotten older, I've realized that adults are nothing more than big kids.

We love getting attention too. Actively listening to anyone you are talking to is a great way to give them this attention.

So, what is active listening?

Active listening is a way of paying attention. It's fully concentrating on, engaging in, and absorbing what someone else is saying to you. It's displaying the obvious and genuine signs such as eye contact and reinforcing responses. This includes nodding, agreeing with "Yes," and asking related questions for clarification.

Active listening can play an important role in helping you grow your business. It's also a skill that can be acquired and developed with some patience and practice.

Here are three reasons why active listening should be a top skill for entrepreneurs:

**1. Earn the trust and respect of your prospective clients.**

The fast-paced entrepreneurial world is often fueled by stress and pressure. Most people appreciate speaking to a supportive and understanding vendor.

Others will find great value in having a person around who reaches out and shows understanding. For example, knowing and acknowledging some of the work-related or personal issues that they face will make them feel valued. This will likely inspire confidence, and they will want to do business with you.

**2. Understand issues and formulate better solutions.**

When you're actively engaged and listening to your prospects concerns, you gain a better understanding of the problem. Then you can subsequently formulate the best solution to bring them on board as a paying client.

We've all been on a sales call with a potential client where our thoughts have gone off on a tangent. Then, when it comes time to close the deal, you may not be able to offer them the most optimal solution. That's why active listening can help you work efficiently, display a sharp intellect, and increase your revenue in the long run.

**3. Active listening can help you defuse conflict.**

There are times in the workplace when you may have to deal with conflict. Although you may not always agree with others' opinions, it's important to be open to perspectives of your employees and colleagues.

Conflict between two parties can make people defensive. But, if a person feels that their concerns are being listened to and taken seriously, the chances of landing a resolution is high.

In addition to the benefits listed above, being an active listener conveys good character, care, and commitment. This contributes to respect in your industry as a thought leader.

## Bella's Story – Breaking My First Board

(As Told by Her Daddy)

One unfortunate thing Bella inherited from me is having very high expectations of yourself – and being very hard on yourself when you fail.

If left unchecked, this causes us to fear trying new things because failing hurts so bad.

Bella ran into this during her first year in karate.

During her first lesson on board breaking, she was having trouble. All the other kids in the class had been in karate longer than her, were older and bigger.

She was very frustrated that she couldn't break the board. Her little eyes started to water, and she wanted to quit.

Her Sensei persuaded her to go back and try a few more times. But she had given up out of pure embarrassment of failing in front of the whole class.

She ran to me in tears and she wanted to go home.

I asked her why she was so sad.

She wouldn't even talk about the failure to break the board. She just said that she wanted to go home.

I began to ask more leading questions to get her to talk about how she felt about not breaking the board.

I explained, "The other kids have all done this several times before, and they had trouble the first time too. And did you know that it's really good that you didn't break it yet? "

"Why, Daddy?"

"Because when you have a hard time doing something you really want to do, and then finally do it...you will be super happy. I know you can do it, Bella. Let's both go out there together. I'll stand right beside you. Listen to Sensei and do your best. No matter what happens, I'll be happy and very proud of you for trying again."

"OK, Daddy."

We went back up, and she tried again.

Didn't break. She wasn't hitting with her first two knuckles.

Tried again.

Didn't break. She wasn't turning her waist and pivoting her back foot.

I could tell she was starting to lose confidence again. I instantly saw myself at age and knew the exact pain she was experiencing. That everyone in the room is judging you. That you will never do it, and are the only person ever to have failed this much.

I gave her arm a reassuring squeeze and gave her a thumbs up (our signal for "I'm proud what you are doing right now.")

Tried again.

Broke it.

The dojo erupted in cheers from all the students, parents, and staff. I picked her up and tossed her in the air to celebrate. She gave my neck a huge squeeze. Her little face was beaming with pride.

After class, we went to get ice cream and talked about how doing hard things isn't always fun at the time, but feels really good after you do it.

We talk about this event every time she gets down on herself and wants to quit something hard.

## The Lesson

Kids learn in school that failing is bad, but successful entrepreneurs understand that failure is an essential part of success.

We've failed so much in our careers and come out on top after, that we forget what it was like when failure hurt so much.

You have to remember to take a step back and teach kids to use failure as a way to continually try to improve.

Turning failures into learning opportunities is not just about saying, "You didn't break the board today, but that's okay."

Instead, encourage them to innovate by embracing a growth mindset: "Okay, so you failed this time -- but what did you learn from it? What would you change tomorrow?"

If they learn it's not alright to fail, or that failure is permanent, they'll be scared to take chances and to think outside the box and try new things.

Essentially, their ability to make their lives better will become increasingly limited.

Conversely, if they view failures as challenges and chances to devise new strategies, they'll become more confident and well-rounded.

The takeaway is that when your child is struggling with something or has setbacks, don't focus on their abilities, focus on what they can learn from it.

## About Brian Ainsley Horn

Bestselling author, investor and entrepreneur, Brian Ainsley Horn, helps professionals leverage their knowledge to gain authority status in their industry, then uses "Authority Marketing" to get them national media exposure.

His unique method has been talked about and covered on The Howard Stern Show, Wall Street Journal, ABC, Perez Hilton, CBS, Forbes, Advertising Age and dozens of other media outlets. Inc Magazine even named Brian an "emerging business leader to watch."

Brian is a contributing writer for Entrepreneur Magazine, The Huffington Post, The Good Men Project, AllBusiness.com and Addicted2Success.

He is also an in-demand speaker that has traveled the world entertaining and educating audiences.

Brian is a devoted Christian, proud father to two amazing kids and an advocate for children with Down syndrome.

**Facebook**
Facebook.com/Brian.Horn

**LinkedIn**
LinkedIn.com/in/BrianAinsleyHorn

**Instagram**
Instagram.com/BrianHorn

**Twitter**
Twitter.com/BrianHorn

## About Bella Horn

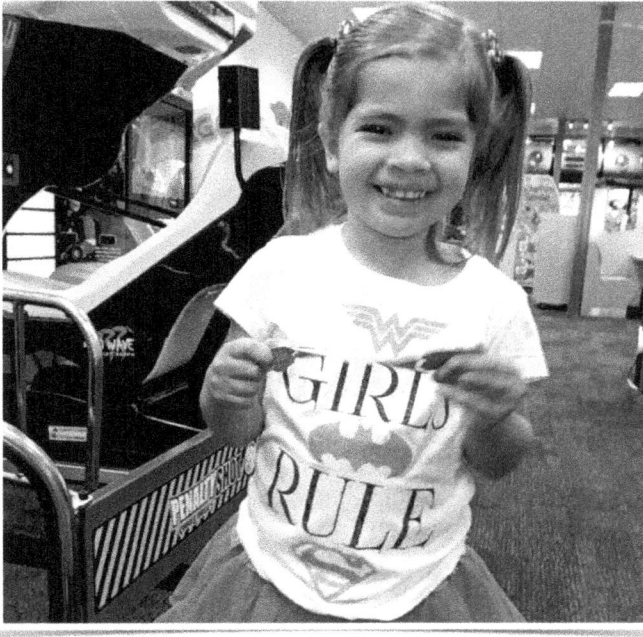

Bella Horn is a Kindergartener at Pomona Elementary. Her favorite subjects are science and recess. Bella loves all the Disney princesses, Supergirl, Wonder Woman and Owlette from PJ Masks. She also does an amazing job helping take care of her brother, Jackson and pet Pomeranian, Koy.

# The Deceptively Powerful Art of Minding Your Own Business

## Carmen's Story

A month had passed since my husband with whom I shared my life for 15 years and the father of my precious baby woke up one morning, demanded a divorce without warning, and instantly wiped out the only world I knew.

My priority was to make every day as smooth and positive as possible for Joshua Gabriel, my wide-eyed five-year-old son, but my mind was constantly in chaos from the noise of well-meaning people. "What did you do to make him cheat on you?" "Maybe if you weighed less/more..." "He was probably bored of you." "Have you considered breast implants?" "What a shame. Every boy needs a dad." I was trying desperately to keep from drowning in my pain but found myself repeatedly pulled back under out of exhaustion and defeat.

*"OMG I suck... I need to lose weight, get a boob job, learn to become more fun, and quickly find Joshua a new dad because whatever I do on my own – as I am – will never be enough to make my poor little boy happy."*

One evening, I was helping Joshua prepare for bed when I began to cry... "I promise to do my very best to fix our family, and we'll be ok just like we were before, so please hang in there." My five-year-old looked at me with his big, sweet eyes and said, *"Mommy, this IS our family... you and me. THIS is our life. You're doing perfect!"*

Leave it to a five-year-old to simplify a traumatic life event like this. After all, he didn't have 15 years of invested time, effort, and have his heart violently stripped away like I did. But my son's innocent wisdom was what I needed at that exact time to begin pulling myself out of the tornado of damaging thoughts that prevented me from moving forward.

## The Lesson

I've come to realize that challenges I face are ALWAYS JUST AS BAD as I make them out to be at any given moment.

Human beings were programmed to anticipate that things are worse than they actually are. Our ancestors from 10,000 years ago had to remain on high alert to every sight, sound, smell, and movement to keep their tribes from being devoured by saber tooth tigers.

So, you see, worrying and being paranoid about the worst-case scenario was meant to be helpful... it's what kept us alive! It is the initial response to finding solutions to problems: "Shoot! My plans have failed. This sucks, and my career is going to be ruined! I need a 'Plan B (or C, D... Z)' fast, and I have to follow it completely through before it's too late to recover!"

But here's how many of us screw this up:

1. We trick ourselves into believing just the act of worrying *in itself* will solve problems. We set our worry-thoughts on loop without actually finding solid solutions that's needed to begin taking action.

2. We open ourselves up to feedback that adds absolutely nothing to help us improve, and pile them on top of our other unhelpful stress-thoughts and believe this added pressure is a sign we're "doing something." *Don't you fall for this like I did... "doing something" is not the same as "getting stuff done."*

3. We get ourselves even more worked up and burnt out by muddying our brains with "why it happened," how we think "it should've happened," or what this could possibly "mean" - instead of remaining clear headed and seeing things as they are, so we can quickly get back on track.

4. We overcomplicate the situation at hand... then procrastinate. We fool ourselves into thinking we have to immediately address and fix everything thrown our way all at once, then we become overwhelmed and discouraged so we put it off because we're tired and sad or not ready... and days, weeks, months, and even years later, *nothing has changed - or maybe gotten worse.*

If only we approached the problems with effective actions, put blinders on to keep out the distraction, and gotten to work regardless of how crappy we feel about life; we'd probably be free and clear on the other side already.

Yep, the life I knew was flushed down the toilet and my mind and heart was a complete mess... but if I were to even BEGIN making any progress at all, I had to force myself to focus *exclusively* on the things I can do to make certain my son was healthy, happy, and safe – and then get off my bum to actually do it. Beating myself up about my weight, the size of my chest, morphing into a party girl, or freaking out about future relationships was not going to bring security and joy into my child's life. What those things did however, was confuse and discourage, drain energy, and wasted several MONTHS of my life that I could've used working on getting stronger and getting back on track.

*"Mommy, this IS our family... you and me. THIS is our new life."* My five-year-old nailed it. I was getting in my own way by not having a solid plan and allowing myself to be distracted by every little thing thrown my way. When all I should've focused on was my very complete family right in front of me: Joshua and Carmen.

1. Take stock of the ACTUAL situation. See things just as they are... not how you think it should be or wish it was.

2. Decide where you'd rather be, create a clear plan of action to get there, and promise yourself to see it all the way through.

3. Until you get yourself out of the hole, focus EXCLUSIVELY on taking effective action and controlling only what is in your power: your thoughts, feelings, actions, and responses. Everything else is irrelevant.

4. Block out energy-wasting distractions such as other people's expectations, hang-ups, and preferences. If you don't, you will be disturbed by the most insignificant comments, reactions, whispers, and disapproving facial expressions directed at you.

5. Only take action where it will be effective (#3). Don't waste your energy (#4).

6. Keep in mind that not seeing immediate results does not equal failure. Stay focused on what's directly in front of you because taking small, calculated steps will get you to your goal faster than giving up due to impatience and frustration.

Of course, being that you're not a robot, it's important to take time to feel your emotions and sort out your thoughts because suppressing your pain can fester into serious damage. Just don't get stuck there. Vent, kick a wall, talk to a therapist or coach, give yourself three days to mope around and cry, then roll your sleeves up and get back to work because this is not where you want to remain.

Finally, I've found that the most effective way to get past difficult challenges is to use the situation to help others. How can family, friends, and clients who might find themselves in a similar place benefit from what I've been dragged through? It almost instantly snaps me out from getting caught up in my own suffering because I become too focused on helping others overcome and heal.

*Til this day, I continue to thank my son for being my special angel ... and he still looks at me with his big, sparkly eyes, wraps me up in a giant hug, and tells me, "I love you, mom."*

## Joshua's Story

*Protect your choices (or you're the one who will live what you ultimately follow through.)*

When I was in kindergarten, I was given a box of Legos containing over 1200 pieces to build the most awesome Star

Wars character. I had much bigger plans though; I was going to design and build a "Super Hyper Power-Force Galaxy" space ship with it.

As I focused on what I felt was the coolest project I've ever committed to in the entire five years I've been on this earth so far, several adults asked why my creation greatly deviated from the picture on the Lego box. *"I'm building something better!"* I proudly answered. "But you should build what the box says you're supposed to build," they replied.

Just when I was about to cater to the masses and take it all apart, my mother wrapped her arms around me and asked, *"These are your blocks, Joshua... we'll display your creation in your room and YOU get to enjoy it for as long as you want... so... what do YOU want to build?"* "A Super Hyper Power-Force Galaxy space ship!!!" I answered excitedly.

And build I did. It took me two days to complete and it was the most magnificent piece of genius I've ever brought into reality at the time. My creation made me feel immensely accomplished and I kept returning to admire my awesome spaceship displayed at the top of my toy shelf!

*My blocks. My room. I get to choose what I will be looking at every day.*

## The Lesson

When I shared my plans on becoming a cardiac surgeon with my family, many quickly pointed out, "Oh, you'll be in school for such a long time! You should pursue (blah, blah) instead." This isn't an impulse decision; I've wanted to become a doctor since I was three years old, so of course, I'm aware of what it's going to take to reach my goal. I've been ready!

At first when people were insistent and as-a-matter-of-factly about THEIR plans for MY future, I found myself questioning my decision. What if they're right? I mean, they're adults with life experiences; while here I am, just a kid. So, I ran those outside opinions through some key questions I've learned from my mom, in order to re-anchor my feet firmly to the ground:

1. Does the outside feedback help me get closer to MY goals or improve as an individual?

2. Are they simply expressing THEIR personal preference/communicating how uncomfortable my choices make them?

3. Are my thoughts and actions negatively affecting the well-being of another person? (others disapproving or feeling disappointed does not count as their "wellbeing")

Answering these questions has saved me from entertaining guilt trips, being talked out of my well thought out decisions, and being pressured into meeting someone else's expectations about my life.

After all, if I listened to what other people wanted for me and became an accountant or an office manager instead, I will be the one stuck living my life doing something I absolutely do not enjoy. Not them. We all view the world around us based on our individual experiences throughout life and how they have shaped us. Other people's hang-ups and preferences (as opposed to solid lessons) are irrelevant in how I want to design my life. I get to practice my freedom to fill my life with my own experiences... so it is my responsibility to protect my choices.

*My time and effort. My life. I get to choose how I live and experience it every day.*

Of course, it's an ongoing lesson. There are times I share my choices with my mom, and after some thought, she suggests a slight variation of it. I refuse, stick with my decision... and receive my mom's usual response, "Ohhh-kaaay... Remember, you're responsible for this." Within minutes, I realize mom's way is (slightly) better... and I get the usual reply, "Now you know!" The point is, I get to choose, I'm given the responsibility to own it, and if all goes as I expected, it builds/enforces my self-confidence, and I feel happy and fulfilled... if it doesn't, I learn from it so I can choose better next time.

I am now sixteen years old and have started my first year of college. My goal is to become a highly respected cardiac surgeon and use my knowledge, skills, and gifts to help heal those suffering from heart conditions... and be rewarded with a healthy income.

P.S. I still enjoy creating a variety of Super Hyper Power-Force Galaxy spaceships from time to time.

## About Carmen Sakurai

Carmen is a Life Strategist, Teacher, Entrepreneur, and Best Selling Author with over 20 years of education and experiences in Stress/Burnout Prevention, Mental Decluttering, and Breakup Recovery. Her solid action steps help her clients get unstuck from what's weighing them down, clear their head, and re-energize so they can live a life they love waking up to.

She is also a contributor at several parenting and lifestyle sites and her articles can be found on Ricky Martin's Piccolo Universe, LittleThings, SheKnows, and Lifehack.

Carmen volunteers as a 1st and 2nd grade Religious Education teacher and fills her free time making pretty food, being hilarious on her mommy blog, and sipping on bubble tea. She currently resides in Las Vegas, NV with her son Joshua and their cat Jordyn.

## Websites

CarmenSakurai.com
ScienceOfClarity.com
MarketingChick.com
NinjaMomDiaries.com
GirlPlusFood.com

## Facebook
Facebook.com/CarmenSakurai

## Twitter
Twitter.com/CarmenSakurai

## Instagram
Instagram.com/Carmen.Sakurai

Instagram.com/TheGirlPlusFood

## LinkedIn
LinkedIn.com/in/CarmenSakurai

## About Joshua Sakurai-Maranon

Joshua is a 16-year-old full-time college student pursuing his goal of becoming a successful cardiac surgeon. He has been a Straight-A student all his life and a member of the National Honor Society since the 6th grade.

He volunteers as a 1st and 2nd grade Religious Education Teacher's Aide and enjoys good food, digital illustration, studying human behavior, martial arts, piano, and discovering simple ways to generate extra income online

**Websites**

TheJoshuaGabriel.com
StuffWeTried.com

# Hustling Runs in Our DNA

## Ryan's Story

I am a father of three boys. One is six, one is five, and the other is six months old. My oldest is starting to pick up on the business thing. For as long as he's been alive, I've run my own business, and for the most part, worked from home. He's come to all our seminars and other events, and if you ask him, "What do you want to be when you grow up?" He'll say, "I want to be a closer."

I'm always trying to teach my oldest son, Jax, the ways of the world in different ways, in different capacities, because I know that he's curious. The other day, he came to me, and he said, "Dad, are we rich? People are saying that we're rich." I had to explain to him exactly what rich meant and why would people even care about that in the first place, and I had to teach him that lesson. One of the most important lessons, not just in business but also in life, that I've shared with him in recent times is, across the street from our house, there's about a 200-acre nature reserve called, Arbor Hills.

Throughout that nature reserve, there are more trails than you could even. It's a fun place to go jogging or mountain biking, and part of it is concrete so you can push strollers and stuff like that if you want, or you can go on the off-road trails. Jax and I went out there on a Saturday, just the two of us. We're going to have a good time together, and he tells me, "I want to be the leader, Dad." You see, his younger brother is just a year younger than him, so often they fight back and forth for who's going to be the leader.

If one of them outruns the other one, and gets in front of him, they get mad and push each other. I explained to him that's not what a leader does. A leader doesn't push other people back; he just pushes harder on himself. This time, it's just my son and me, and he's the leader, and obviously, in every way possible, I am superior to him. I have superior intelligence, I'm faster, bigger, stronger, so I keep pushing up on him. Every time he tries to slow down going through the trails, I push up on him and occasionally, I would get in front of him, and cause him to have to speed up and catch up to me, and then I would urge him, and push him with my hand on his back to pass me.

He would fall behind me, and he'd say, "I can't keep up; you're faster than me." I'd reply, "Leaders don't complain when they fall behind. They simply make their way back to the front of the line." That's been an important lesson that I've shared with him over and over. I use that phrase all the time now. It's a metaphor for everything. If you're going to be a business leader, if your competition passes you up, you can't cry about it; you just have to work harder.

I wouldn't allow him to cry about it and complain while we were hiking the trails. I'm not going to stand for that. I'm not raising that type of kid. Instead, I'm teaching him that when you fall behind, you have to push that much further to get ahead. Most fathers would have told their kids, "Hey, it's okay, you can sit down, you can relax, you can take a break." But I know the game of life doesn't have breaks, and I know that he's either going to learn the hard way, or he can learn throughout these experiences.

I also know that leadership is not something that you're simply given, and I wanted him to understand that as well. Leadership is not just something that you ask somebody, "Can you be the leader," and they agree to it. That's some schoolyard stuff, that's not how the real world works. In the real world, you have to step up and become the leader, and if the leader should arise, then the followers will arrive. You have to become that leader. I wanted to instill that in him, if you're going to lead in sports, if you're going to lead in business, if you're going to lead in the schoolyard, if you're going to lead in the market place, then what you need to be doing is leading yourself to push harder than the guy next to you; that's what leaders do.

## The Lesson

Think about how you could apply this in your life. Right now, the competition might be smoking you, and you might be in a situation where you've spent all this time working on sales funnels and marketing plans, and sales execution processes, and you've thought of everything, and you've put all this stuff together and it's just not working out for you and you're getting your ass whipped. You need to remember, if you're going to be a market place leader, then you can't complain when you fall behind; you have to work twice as hard to get back up to the front of the line.

If you're a leader in the market place, know that somebody else wants to be a leader too, and it's going to be a constant struggle. For example, look at Apple and Samsung, Apple is a leader, but Samsung every day is taking a little bit of market share, working a little bit harder, and hoping Apple's latest launch fails. The competition is always going to be there, and if you're going to be a leader, embrace the competition. Know that it exists, know that it's going to be there, and keep pushing past it, no matter what.

## Jax's Story

A few days later, my son said to me, "Dad, I want to start a business." I thought, "Well, that's an interesting phrase for a six-year-old to say." He said, "I want to buy fidget spinners, and I want to sell them." This was a proud dad moment for me, and I thought, "Now you're speaking my language." So, I taught him about investment capital, and I told him, "I'm the bank. I've got the money, and I'm going to loan you $20 to buy five fidget spinners, but I expect you to pay me $25 back."

I planned to use the $25 to buy six fidget spinners, but he didn't know that yet. We hadn't got that far in the lesson. I said, "Five fidget spinners and I'm going to loan you $20, but you owe me $25 back," and he asked, "Well, will you tell me how to count money?" I said, "Absolutely," and I explained to him what a $5 bill looked like because that's what he needed to collect to sell a fidget spinner.

I showed him what a $5 bill looks like, and I said, "You sell them to your friends for this. Now here is what you do: go to school and you tell your friends you have these really cool fidget spinners." We bought some American Flag fidget spinners right around Memorial Day. "Tell them they're called 'Freedom Spinners.' Take them to school and show them to your friends, but don't let them take the spinners home. Tell them to bring five dollars back tomorrow, and you'll sell them your Freedom Spinner."

He went to school with all five Freedom Spinners. When he came home that evening, he didn't have any Freedom Spinners.

I was expecting $25. The loan is due, the product is gone, it's time to re-up. "So, Jax, did you sell any Freedom Spinners today?" "I sold them all dad, every one of them. All of them." "Do you have my money?" "Oh, no. No, they told me they would give me the money." "Okay, okay. Well, we're going to get it tomorrow buddy."

The next day after school, I asked, "Hey buddy, did you get the money?" Jax replied, "I didn't want to ask them. I just let them have them."

I said, "Well, the bank wants their money back," and I explained to him, "What if I borrowed that money from somebody and now I owe them $25, and I don't have it because I thought you were going to pay it." He looked at that moment, and he realized, "Oh, what if my dad didn't give me that money and he did borrow it from somebody else?" I taught him about our agreement. "Our agreement was our word, that I was going to loan you some money, and this is the first time in your life son, that I've ever loaned you money, and you come back empty handed, and you cost me the money, because we don't have any products we can sell any more."

He said, "Well, they are my friends, and I just wanted them to be happy." I said, "That's absolutely okay. You know you could have come to me and asked me to buy toys for your friends, and I would've probably done that for you too, but instead, you wanted to go into business, and business isn't about friends. Business is about making money, and we got these Freedom Spinners so that we can make some money. So, what are we going to do about this?" He said, "Maybe we should order some more." I said, "Do you have more people to sell to?" He said, "No. I gave them all to my friends. I don't have any more friends that I want to give them to."

Finally, I asked, "Well, do you have any more friends that you'd think would buy them?" When he responded, "I don't know," that was the end of our business ventures, so far.

## The Lesson

The lesson to you is that a lot of people get caught up in the 'Homeboy Hookup.' You know how you see in the car business, guys come in, they wouldn't make any money off their friends. These weren't even their friends; they were just acquaintances that they hadn't seen since high school; give them the Homeboy Hookup.

People hit me up for stuff all the time, "Hey man, well, let me get the Homeboy Hookup." The Homeboy Hookup will make you go broke, and my son realized that. His first business venture failed, six years old. He borrowed money from the bank, failed miserably, all because of the Homeboy Hookup. If you have people in your life that are trying to discount your services, trying to get your stuff for free, they're no different than these toddlers that took the Freedom Spinners from my son with no intention of paying him. Be proud of the fees that you charge, and be proud of the way that you run your business and the way you conduct yourself.

Don't lower your standards or your fees for anybody, even if they're a Homeboy. Because I can tell you, every time that you lower the price, you end up like my son. Every time that you hook somebody up, you end up like my son; you're the one that's out of luck, stuck holding the debt.

## About Ryan and Jax Stewman

A BAMF, unafraid to take action, Ryan Stewman, aka the "Hardcore Closer," is a 4x bestselling author, podcaster and blogger. Best known for consulting with Alpha media types on rapidly growing their sales via the use of powerful advertising and marketing, Ryan is a salesman turned CEO. He has not had a salaried job his entire life. He's mastered the art of super effective communication and has closed more transactions than he has time to count. With his no-BS approach to strategizing and scaling businesses, Ryan has helped high-net worth performers adjust their business plans resulting in windfall profits.

After gaining prolific social media experience, Ryan decided to teach people from all sales fields and industries how to sell online and Hardcore Closer was born. In the first year, HC closed over $150K in gross sales; the second year, HC hit over $300K; and in 2016, HC generated over $2M.

His notoriety and savage sales acumen have put him on the pages of the largest media publications on the planet. He contributes to and has been featured in Forbes, Entrepreneur, Addicted2Success, The Good Men Project, The Lighter Side of Real Estate and Huffington Post in addition to other top-tier sites.

He states the key to his success is taking action and working hard.

Hardcore Closer is an online learning resource for salespeople, selling e-learning products in the advertising, marketing funnel sales and social media arenas and offers personal coaching and live events. Break Free Academy is Hardcore Closer's flagship program and provides every tool needed to market businesses online and crush the competition.

Ryan was born and raised in Texas. He's a doting husband and proud father to three sons. He and his family live in Dallas.

Subscribe to his blog at HardCoreCloser.com

# My Kids Are Not My "Why"

## Jody's Story

I started my first business, a web design company, when I was 21. I was never really cut out for being an employee.

I was a sink and swim learner and got very good at what I did. However, due to some really stupid financial decisions, I was close to bankruptcy in my twenties, not once but twice.

I was one of the youngest to win a place in the *Business Women of the Year* awards, and stupidly thought that fame and publicity would last forever.

Sales went through the roof, and I had a sudden growth burst like never before.

Being an ego-driven 20-something-year-old, I used the financial gains to do things like over-commit to employees (instead of contractors) and big leases, plus all the costs that come with that, as if the sales boom would just continue.

It didn't, and I nearly lost everything.

At 29, I became *surprise pregnant* with my daughter.

Suddenly everything changed.

It was not about me anymore. There was an actual human that would be watching my every move. This was so much bigger than me and my childish ego.

At that moment, I reassessed everything.

There were two big questions that I asked myself that completely changed what I was doing.

1.  What have you done in the past in your business that has worked?

    Do more of that!

2.  What have you done in your business that has NOT worked?

    NEVER do those things again!

I was sitting at my desk when my water broke. The contractions had not started, so I figured I could at least smash out these last two websites before I went into labour.

Six hours later, I had nailed the two websites. I stood up from my desk and instantly went into labour.

Before I knew it, I was holding my daughter in my arms swearing I would never ever work my ass off doing those ridiculous hours, draining my soul at my desk day in and day out.

I would learn to delegate and automate in my business like a champion, and I would delete any tasks that were not moving me towards making money.

I was convinced that making money was crucial to give my daughter the life she deserved.

Things were never going to be the same again.

I could no longer afford to make silly financial decisions or party my life away. I was responsible for another human!

I had found my WHY.

At least I thought I had.

Fast forward five years.

I had chosen to go it alone and was now a single mum with my five-year-old daughter Milly and three-year-old son Joey.

They were good kids but there were still times I would hide in the pantry and cry so that they wouldn't see me.

I was making more money than I had ever made in my life. I was surrounded by the right people. I was pumped in my business. Clients were happy, and I was on fire in my business financially. I was loving it.

Yet, I still felt unfulfilled. I couldn't work it out. I finally had everything I wanted, but it didn't feel right. I was out of alignment somewhere.

Then it hit me.

My kids were no longer my WHY.

They were no longer a driver for me to build my business and make money. I felt this terrible sense of parent guilt.

It was not because they were not my number one priority; they were and always will be.

I had just come to realise that a three- and five-year-old don't give a shit about money!

We could have been living in a tin shed in the ghetto, and they wouldn't care.

We could have lived in a mansion in the hills, and they wouldn't give a shit!

All that my kids ever really needed from me was my love and my time.

## The $15,000 Lesson

In that first year on our own, I took them to Singapore for 10 days for fun. The trip cost around $15,000.

We went to Universal Studios and the Singapore Zoo. We stayed at the beautiful W Resort on Sentosa Island. We even visited a massive toy store where I spoiled them rotten.

Everything we wanted was at our finger tips! I mean that literally. The W Resort had a button on the phone that said, "Whatever you want, whenever you want it."

As we travelled home, I asked Milly and Joey what they loved the most about the trip. Their answers...

Milly: "I loved eating out at restaurants every meal."

Joey: "I loved swimming in the pool."

No mention of the Zoo, or the rides at Universal Studios, or the toys.

What this experience taught me was even more than ever that the best way to grow my business was not focus on making money.

My "job" was to serve my family the best way I could through serving my clients, and the best way to do that was LEVERAGE. I even made a short film with that title.

It didn't matter how much money I made if I didn't have the time to spend with my kids. When I was with my kids, I needed to have my business set up so I could be 100% present.

It was time to double down on those three keys again.

Automate, Delegate, and Delete any tasks that were not keeping me in my flow.

I STILL teach my clients deeper versions of those strategies today, a decade later.

Every month, I like to ask myself those questions. What is working and what isn't, and to constantly tweak what I am automating and delegating.

I interviewed my daughter as part of a launch video once and here is what she said:

"I like your job because in the mornings at Dad's house, he has already gone to work when I wake up, and I don't get to say goodbye. Nana has to be there. When we are with you, you're home all the time and get to be there to get us after school. We don't get that at Dad's house."

I especially love this because I do travel a lot, but I do it when they are at their Dad's house. I get the best of both worlds.

Joey said, "When you have a business and not a job, you don't have to go to work. You can just do what you want."

That sounds pretty awesome to me!

In summary...

If your business feels HARD and you're not in a state of flow each day, you need to ask the what is and isn't working questions more often. If not, then you'll forever be a slave to your business.

It's about constantly taking the actions that move you closer to your ultimate lifestyle.

My kids taught me that lifestyle ALWAYS need to come first, no matter what.

## Building Confidence in Your Kids

My daughter seems to have natural entrepreneurial skills. She's always looking for new ideas and how she can turn anything into content or money.

My son has my stubborn determination and a constant need to win.

One thing is for sure. When it comes to my kids, it is a case of "Monkey see—Monkey do." They don't miss a beat! Often, they'll use my own lines on me. Perhaps they are a little TOO smart. ;)

Video is a massive part of my business. It always has been. When I do more videos, sales increase. If I'm not consistent, sales die off.

I absolutely LOVE doing video. It's fun and something I could do all day long that would never feel like work. Especially if there is comedy involved.

Milly did her first video at four years old after watching me film a series of blog posts. She made videos about manners and washing your hands. They were super cute.

By the age of five, she was drawing my program logos all over books and the whiteboards around the house.

When Milly asked if she could start her own YouTube channel for her and Joey, I was excited to get to come up with a brand and help them pull it all together.

However, given that my daughter is cut from the same cloth as me and bossy as hell... she had already come up with a name.

"The BYT Show" which stood for *The Best YouTubers*. I was pretty impressed.

I thought I could use my Photoshop skills to at least design them a logo.

NOPE! Milly said, "I want the logo to come from me and I will draw it and you can scan it."

Shot down again mum.

Here is the bit that impressed me the most.

I had a program called *Online TV Pro* which taught people how to create their own TV show using YouTube. One module was about how to structure your video content in five phases.

When I explained to the kids how they should structure the show with and intro and call to action etc., they stopped me in my tracks. "We know. We know."

I filmed their first show for them and I was in shock.

They had practiced a joint intro including their names and brand of their show.

They clarified what the viewer was going to get out of watching the show.

They delivered it with such engaging character that I was in awe.

At the end, they not only asked people to subscribe but they also asked questions and asked them to share their answer in the comments to engage with their audience.

It bought a tear to my eye.

I recently asked the kids what it is about video and business that they have learned over the years.

Here are the kids' explanations:

Joey: "You tell people in movies about your life and how you live."

Milly: "You answer people's questions by making videos. Then they go and do what you say, and if they have any more troubles they ask you and you can tell them what next to do. So, then they get to have a better life, do better things, and do smarter things. Your business is good because you get to help people and put comedy in it to make a sad thing happy."

I then asked the kids what it was about video that helped them in their lives. Here is what they said:

Joey: "When I was four and a half and we started a YouTube channel, we opened Shopkins. I was excited but didn't want to say much. Then I watched Mummy and YouTubers and started to see how they laugh and act on video. That made me learn what I needed to do on my videos. Then I did more than I was before because I was getting used to it.

Milly: "Joey seemed shy at the start, but then he got more confident in his videos. He got good at sharing his emotions."

Joey piped up in agreement, "Doing videos made us more confident and show our emotions better basically"

I've watched these kids and their videos develop over the years and each time they get a little bit more confident to open up more.

Milly and Joey don't even realize yet that in their own growth they have also learned, without knowing, video structure and strategy.

## The Lesson

In all my years of working with entrepreneurs, the biggest hurdle we come across is their fear of being on camera. If it's not that, it's how they are like robots and allow the camera to strip them of their personality because they are worried about how they look.

Getting to watch the confidence unfold in my two kids is something I know will carry them a long way in their futures.

Even their teachers have said they both nailed their Google Docs presentations and are confident in front of the class.

I strongly believe that self-love and being 100% yourself is the key to your happiness.

This is what Milly and Joey have developed from creating videos for the last three years.

I couldn't be prouder and I'm excited to watch what greatness it brings for them throughout their lives :)

## About Jody Jelas

Jody is often referred to as "The most transparent and authentic in the business."

Jody is the Author of "LadyBalls" which hit the best seller list on the first day it hit Amazon. She helps women smash past their blocks and rock out a life that is far beyond what they ever dreamed of with her LadyBalls Retreats and programs.

Jody also helps men and women Coaches, Teachers and Entrepreneurs create an authentic online brand through video by being their 100% non-filter selves! She then helps them to extract their best knowledge and turn it into an online leveraged programs.

Over the last 19 years, she has helped top business folk and online marketers grow their brand globally and develop a leveraged business through strategies and most importantly MINDSET.

Jody is from New Zealand and has been a star-making Online Entrepreneur from a young age. She went to her first personal development training at the age of 14 and started her first business when she was just 21 and has been self-employed ever since. She was also one of the youngest "Business Women of the Year" Awards-Finalists ever!

She is passionate about helping people kick their life to another level through tried and tested strategies and personal development. She has worked with and MasterMinds with top online marketers and personal development gurus from all over the world her entire life and loves nothing more than to watch her clients evolve into the most epic version of themselves.

**Facebook**
Facebook.com/IAmJodyJelas

**Instagram**
Instagram.com/JodyJelas

**Videos**
JodyJelas.com

**Find out more about the LadyBalls Retreats**
LadyBallsRetreat.com

**Download free trainings**
CoolStuffFromJodz.com

## About Milly Tolhopf and Joey Tolhopf

Milly and Joey are obsessed with creating YouTube videos and learning from following other YouTubers.

Milly loves to shop like a teenager (even though she is only nine) and is a born entrepreneur. She's always thinking of creative ways to make money so she can spend more time doing the things she loves, especially if it means not having to unload the dishwasher.

Joey is a ball of energy who loves playing rugby, soccer, tag, and touch rugby. He's always caring for everyone around him, and is big on hugging!

They both love living a lifestyle of VIP travel and are two of the most compassionate kids you will meet.

# There's Always Enough

## Victor's Story

When my son, Aaron, was young, I started doing real estate. I was just learning about real estate, turning and burning contracts, and flipping houses for money. The work was just an ATM for me; I was taking cash when I needed it. I don't think I really grasped the concept of real estate from a business perspective.

One night I came home after a long day. I was still really new in real estate, and I had gone all day without eating because I was busy doing a bunch of stuff and had completely forgotten to stop to eat. As soon as I got home, I went to the kitchen and made a sandwich. I used the last, butt end of the bread and the last pieces of ham and cheese.

I sat down on the couch to eat my sandwich and Aaron came running out of the back room and said "Baby!" At the time, he hadn't started calling me "Daddy" because his mom called me "Baby." So, he said, "Baby! Baby!" and hugged me.

He looked at me, looked at the TV, and then looked at my sandwich and asked, "Can I have that?" Even though I was hungry, I handed him the sandwich and said, "Yeah, go ahead." He ate while I sat there with him. For the first time as an adult, I knew that now I had a responsibility to myself and my kids.

The realization spilled over into the business that I was in, too. I had to not just look at myself, what I can eat, how much money I can make. I was now responsible for other people's livelihoods and providing for them. And I started taking it seriously, not just for my own life, and the changes I had to make as a person, but also for my son.

I decided, "He's going to come first. If you're going to be in this business, your clients are going to come first, your tenants are going to come first, your responsibilities are going to come first. Everything has to go that way. And if you don't do that, you will never eat."

Aaron ate part of the sandwich and gave me the rest. And that was enough to fulfill me even though before I thought I needed the whole thing.

## The Lesson

This was really the first conscious moment that it wasn't just about me eating anymore; it was about everybody who was relying on me to show up and be a provider for them.

I understood that if I was going to actually succeed at anything, I needed to take a step back and start asking, "How could this work for other people? How could this not just be about Victor?"

That really helped me throughout my career because I stopped looking at, "How can I get all of the money? All of the profit?" And I started saying, "Okay, how can I make this work because I have to also provide for my family. There's going to be times when I'm not going to be the person eating first in some of my deals. I need to make sure that my tenants do."

My business partnerships improved because I had a better understanding of what needed to be done, and what was required of me. My employees were getting paid first, and my business was taking care of the things that it needed to.

## Aaron's Story

I have lots of stories with my dad. He has a way of embarrassing me sometimes for the better which has had a big impact on my life by teaching me to show up and be myself. That's impacted me throughout my life in anything I've done, either with business or in sports.

One day we were downtown sitting outside of a Starbucks. It's right in the heart of the city, so there were a lot of people walking around. He had just come from a business meeting, he was all dressed up, and I was wearing some shorts and a tee shirt.

It was real breezy that day. I remember looking behind me through a window glass and there were these two really cute girls that are my age. My dad saw me looking and he said, "Well, say something." I was like, "Nah, nah, nah, I can't because I'm shy." So, my dad knocked on the window, pointed at me and said, "My son likes you!" Then he turned back to me and said, "Now you have to say something."

I thought, "Man. He really did that." I'm nervous, I'm freaking out, I'm thinking I'm going to walk into this Starbucks and these girls are just going to yell a fat "No!" in my face, throw coffee on me, and it's going to be the worst thing ever.

I'm like, "Dad, I don't know what to say." He said, "Dude, just be yourself." So, I got up, I went to the front door, and I opened it.

These girls had their eyes on me from the minute he knocked. I'm like, "Man, this is ... Oh my god." I'm freaking out, my heart's pounding out of my chest. I finally get up and introduce myself, and it ended up being a great time. I got both their phone numbers. They were really cool girls, and I think they were a grade older than me.

## The Lesson

I've never had a problem showing up for something, but I've always been terrified of what's going to happen. The day at the coffee shop really opened my eyes to the fact that things are not always as bad as they seem in your mind as long as you just be yourself.

I've taken that with me in business and sports. One thing I've always gone back to is: Man, show up and just be yourself. Because in doing that, I've been able to give myself a lot of experiences in sales & marketing and wrestling that a lot of people can't say they have. My experiences are unique to me because nobody else can have my experiences.

A few years ago, I was involved in wrestling. The same lesson applies to wrestling: just show up and be yourself. When I was first introduced to proper Roman wrestling, I had only been wrestling for about a year. I was truly an immature wrestler that was only 18 years old amongst men wrestling. And I got my ass handed to me for the entire first semester.

But I kept showing up. I quit worrying about being beat and what others thought. And then next thing you know, over the year, I stopped getting scored on, and I started scoring on people. I was putting my name out there more and more. I eventually graduated from the Olympic training site to the Olympic training center and got to wrestle with some of the best across the world.

## About Victor Bell Jr.

Victor Bell, Jr. (Coach Vic) is the founder of Warhorse Academy and creator of "Champion" – a program committed to helping today's elite businessmen go from good to great to unstoppable in business and life.

To learn more about Coach Vic, visit ChampionArmy.com

Or, follow him at Facebook.com/warhorse.strength

## About Aaron Holland Bell

Aaron Holland Bell is the marketing videos and editing manager for The Academy-Champion program events. Aaron was the top sales professional his field in Colorado Springs.

Aaron competed for the USA Olympic program in Colorado Springs as a Greco Roman wrestler.

# The Yellow School Bus

## Nora's Story

For six years, I spent my morning commute to work counting yellow school buses. My daughter had been obsessed with them since she was tall enough to see out the backseat passenger window.

I honestly didn't understand her fascination with them. To me, school buses were slow, smelled like somebody's abandoned gym locker and weren't very safe (our school system's buses didn't have seat belts). There was no denying how her face lit up whenever she saw one though, so we made it a game to excitedly point them out and count them on the way to drop her off at daycare.

My daughter's interest in yellow school buses didn't wane by the time she started elementary school. In fact, the obsession only grew stronger. Every day she begged and pleaded to take that yellow school bus home, and every day I had to say no. I spent my workday in a corporate office until 5:30 p.m. or later. I was never home when the bus would have dropped her off after school.

This went on for several years. By that time in my life, I had spent 15 years investing myself in a six-figure corporate career.

By every measure of my non-entrepreneurial family and friends, it was a very successful career. I had taken the traditional path I was *supposed to*, the path I was told was the de facto standard of success.

Yes, I followed the progression of Bachelor's degree, Master's degree, and MBA right on up the corporate ladder. But instead of feeling a sense of achievement and happiness, every rung of the ladder only seemed to take me one step further away from who I really was and what (and who) I truly loved.

The truth was, my corporate job left me feeling stressed and empty. To cope, I became an addict, but not to drugs or alcohol. No, I was addicted to buying domain names. I bought hundreds of domains, and I spent hours dreaming up ways I could use them.

I was dissatisfied with my job, and I found myself I spending more and more time doing something I did enjoy - digital marketing. Late nights and early mornings were spent helping everyone I could grow their businesses online.

I spent more and more time trying to balance it all, trying to maintain the corporate life and still feed my creativity and professional drive. I stopped sleeping and consumed far too much caffeine. Thankfully, somewhere in the middle of that, I found my momentum and the spark my life had been missing. Digital marketing was my "yellow school bus."

Digital marketing brought me joy, and I realized it was something I wanted to do every day. But how could I leave a six-figure job without putting my family or my finances at risk? I didn't yet have the courage to follow a non-traditional career path. I didn't know if I ever would.

I'll never forget the day that all changed. It was just another normal day at work. I was in the middle of another waste-of-time morning meeting. As usual, I took out my phone and bought another two domains, FTheMeeting.com and FTheJob.com. For a moment I just sat there, staring through the people around me. *How did I get here?* I wondered. *How have I ended up feeling so empty and disconnected from the life I really want to live?*

At that moment, I knew I needed a change, and I made up my mind. I couldn't keep doing what I was doing. Although I wasn't completely sure how it would look or what I would do, there was one thing I did know: my daughter was riding that yellow school bus home today.

That day, I left work early enough to meet my daughter as she stepped off the bus at the bus stop. I took a picture of her as she stepped off that yellow school bus and ran full speed towards me, smile as wide as a mile, hair streaming behind her. My daughter's dream had come true.

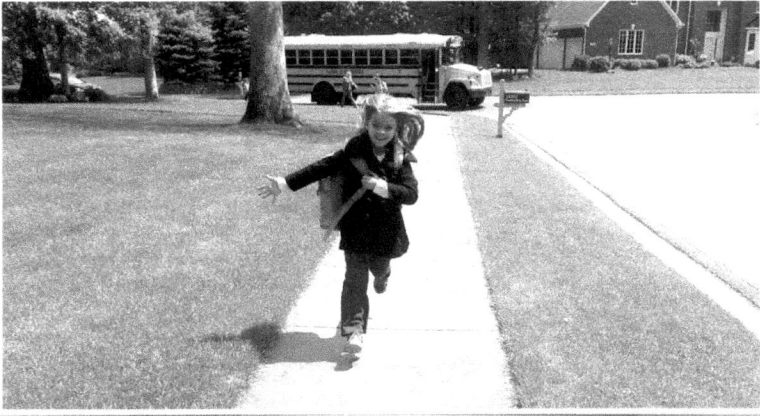

At that moment, I knew two things: my little girl needed to take the bus home more often, and I needed to find that kind of joy in my work. My daughter's relentless dedication to pursuing what she wanted and her joy upon receiving it, gave me the boost I needed to go after my "yellow school bus." It was time for me to create a life where I could spend time doing what I love while serving people I love.

It wasn't easy, but I was relentless, and I shared the entire journey with my kids.

There were moments when voices of doubt chanted inside my head. I didn't hide that from them. If I got knocked down, they saw it, and they were there when I got back up again.

I shared the victories and the wins right along with the battles and defeats. I shared the lessons learned and the things that kept me going. I shared my fears and how I worked past them. I even shared the tears and the lack of sleep.

I wanted my kids to understand the importance of holding on, digging in, and giving something everything they have, even if they're not sure it will work out.

I wanted my kids to understand the reality of the entrepreneurial journey. I needed them to see that the path to achieving something that's important to you isn't always paved with sunshine and butterflies. Unicorns and leprechauns aren't going to show up with pots of gold, and a genie in a bottle isn't going to appear and grant three wishes.

I wanted my kids to understand the importance of relationships. Sharing the journey with them not only forged a very special bond among us, but they were able to watch me develop very special bonds with clients, mentors, and friends.

Through it all, I let my kids see me hustle, let them experience determination and perseverance in action. They were there every step of the way.

I chased my "yellow school bus" dream, and I built a six-figure marketing agency in less than a year and retired from the corporate life. The first day I stayed home, I met my daughter at the bus stop again. I took another picture so I'd always remember that moment.

The joy on her face said it all . . . for both of us.

## The Lesson

The lessons my kids learned through me during this time have been invaluable. Being an entrepreneur in front of your kids teaches them things that they might not learn anywhere else, like:

- Don't be afraid to fail. Failures aren't bad; they're stepping stones to success that, if you're paying attention, can teach you valuable life lessons.

- Keep improving yourself. Don't ever stop wanting to be better.

- Be proactive. Take initiative to solve the issues in front of you, and be resourceful. Those traits make things happen!

- Do not give up on yourself or your dreams. Practice persistence and determination.

It wasn't always easy. Just like I didn't understand my daughter's fascination with that smelly old yellow school bus, most people didn't understand why I would want to leave a "safe" six-figure income for the uncertainty of starting my own business.

It's common for entrepreneurs like me to have friends and family who don't understand the desire to forge a new path. Changing the status quo seems like a daunting task, and working like crazy to make it all happen takes a major investment of time and energy some aren't willing to give.

No, it wasn't easy, but it was worth it. Everyone deserves their version of that yellow school bus, and if you're considering entrepreneurship, here are a few tips I found helpful along the way.

**Run after what it is in your life that brings you joy!** Others may not see the prize like you do, but that doesn't make it any less valuable a journey. If it brings you joy, it's worth it.

**Find a community of like-minded people who will understand and support you!** It can be your family, your kids, your significant other, members of your church, or members of an online group. No matter who it is, find them! They are the people who will not only lift you up and celebrate your wins, but pick you back up and dust you off when you fall.

**Share your journey!** I don't come from a family of entrepreneurs, so it was very important to me to share my journey with my children. By sharing my journey with my kids - the good, the bad and the ugly – I was able to teach them some lessons that will transcend whatever career path they choose.

I kept that picture of my daughter getting off the yellow school bus on my phone for a long time as a reminder to never give up pursuing my yellow school bus.

Your joy may not be riding in a yellow school bus or creating a six- or seven-figure marketing agency so you can work from home and watch your kids get off the bus every day, and that's okay. Whatever that vision of joy is for you, embrace it and share it with the people you love most. You never know whose life you'll change on the way to changing your own.

If you're looking for a mentor or marketing for your own business, please email me at nora@norasudduth.com or visit NoraSudduth.com for more information. I'd love to connect!

## Ryann's Story – Making Space for Something New

Starting something new used to make me feel uneasy. It's hard to not know how to do things that other people seem to have mastered. That changed when my Mom and I started training in taekwondo. We both started as white belts and trained side by side for over three years. Everyone starts as a white belt, but we moved through the different colored belts until we finally earned that first-degree black belt together.

I was selected to be on our taekwondo demonstration "dream team" and the leadership team. I was "all in" (something my Mom says when she's talking about her commitment to something). The opportunities were endless, but something about it bothered me. It didn't leave any time for me to try new things.

I didn't want to let my master instructors down, and I felt pressured into continuing since it was an honor to be selected for the team... but I knew that doing it because I wanted to make others happy or because it was expected of me wasn't the right reason.

I wanted to try new things and have the time and space to do it without pushing the limits and filling every 30-minute window of time with activity. I've seen my mom's schedule at times, and I don't know how she keeps up that pace.

This year I made the decision to not participate in the "dream team" demonstration. While it's truly an honor to be selected for the team, I felt that I wanted to spend that time doing things that were more meaningful to me.

It wasn't an easy decision to make, and I wondered if I was doing the right thing. Some people tried to change my mind about it, but I just knew it wasn't a good fit for me. In the end, I found the confidence to take a different path and make space for other things I wanted to try. I didn't know if I would like them better or enjoy them more than taekwondo, but I wanted the opportunity to see for myself.

It's the same thing with people in your life too. I realized that some of my friends at school weren't always making the best decisions. There was a lot of unnecessary drama, breaking the rules, and talking behind people's backs. I realized how negative and unhappy I felt when I was with this group of friends. I didn't feel like myself. I was stressed out and didn't feel good about myself.

Even though I had been friends with the same group for three years, I decided it was best to leave the group and find new friends to hang out with. It was hard, but I knew it was something I needed to do.

## The Lesson
(as told by Ryann's Mom)

Ryann, like many entrepreneurs I know, tends to be a people pleaser. She doesn't want to let people down, hurt anyone's feelings, or make waves. Too many times she'd go with the flow even if it was taking her away from who she really was and where she wanted to go. Sound familiar?

People pleasers tend to feel guilty when they say no and are familiar with over-commitment and the stress that goes along with saying yes too often. Many entrepreneurs fall into the trap of trying to please everyone, so they take on projects, clients, and activities that don't really align with their priorities, values, and goals. Ultimately, they end up somewhere they never wanted to go.

There are many reasons people say yes when they should say no. Guilt, fear of missing out on a good opportunity, or wanting to prove they can do it all. Whatever the reason, saying yes to too many things that don't align with who you are and who you want to be is just overwhelming and unproductive.

Saying yes to one (or multiple) things almost always means having to say no to something else. Say yes to too many of the wrong things, and you may have to say no to something that's very important – maybe even the ideal opportunity you've been waiting for.

If you're a people pleaser, recognize that you tend to want to say yes when you should say no. Taking the following three steps can help you avoid the stress and overwhelm of over commitment.

## 1. Get crystal clear on your own goals and objectives.

If you have identified your priorities, values, and goals, it will be much simpler to identify which opportunities align and which don't. Stress hits when you get stuck doing things that don't align with who you want to be or what's truly important to you. Beat the stress by having a clear set of goals and objectives already in place.

Priorities and values can shift over time and are shaped by your life events, so it's worth sitting down and taking some time to check in with yourself on a regular basis.

## 2. Simplify your commitments.

If you're already over-committed and stressed out, it's time to make a change. Ask yourself, "Do I enjoy doing this activity?" "Is this activity fulfilling?" "Does this activity help me personally or professionally?" If the answer is no, devise a plan to stop those things as soon as possible.

It is okay to protect yourself. In fact, it's necessary to reach your goals. Learn to say no to the people, activities, and commitments that don't move you toward your goal. In addition, work to avoid distractions and eliminate the guilt-ridden "should do" activities that can easily overtake your schedule.

## 3. Surround yourself with like-minded people.

Who you spend time with influences the person you become, either elevating you or bringing you down. Be mindful of the people you choose to surround yourself with, and be aware of those you let influence your beliefs and behavior.

When Ryann decided to not participate in the demonstration team to create space for other activities, other adults she respected and looked up to made comments and tried to convince her she was making a mistake. I was so incredibly proud when she held her position. And when she opted out of a popular social circle because she didn't like what they did or how they acted? It's a parent's dream come true!

### In Ryann's own words...

It's hard to turn down opportunities, especially when everyone else tells you how lucky you are to have them. You have to be honest with yourself about what YOU want and what's important to YOU no matter what everyone else is telling you. I'm really glad I decided to create more time and space in my life to try new things. I've been able to join a local swimming rec team, started playing the flute and signed up for ice skating lessons, something I wouldn't have had time for otherwise.

Changing friend groups wasn't easy either, but today I have friends who value me for me and don't expect me to be something I'm not. My friends are kind, loving, happy and they don't talk badly about anyone else. I feel so much happier now and love having time to try new things!

## About Nora Sudduth

Nora Sudduth is an expert in marketing that converts and business systems that scale, two disciplines that can generate massive success for business owners and entrepreneurs.

Originally from Chicago, IL, Nora currently lives in Carmel, Indiana with her husband, two children, two dogs and the cat. She's earned her first-degree black belt in taekwondo with her daughter, loves cheering for her son on the soccer and baseball fields, and is a proud supporter of her local humane society.

Nora holds various digital marketing certifications, is a certified project manager and has earned a Bachelor of Science degree in computer science, a Master of Science in engineering psychology, and her MBA. Before striking out on her own, she spent 15 years in corporate America helping companies create and implement technology systems and business processes designed to generate and support exponential growth. She often consults with seven-figure businesses owners who want to scale to eight figures and beyond without the typical business growing pains or impacting their customers' experience.

Every day Nora puts into action the marketing strategies she teaches others to use and apply in their own businesses. Nora has created multi-million dollar programs such as the ClickFunnels® Certified Partner Program and ClickFunnels® ClickStart Program. She also owns and operates Funnel Store, which is her own marketing agency that specializes in sales funnel creation, conversion optimization, and traffic generation.

Nora's love and passion for including her family in her work led to her creation of Funnel Kids, an online learning platform designed to teach children marketing, business and entrepreneurial skills - skills they often don't learn in school.

**For more information, visit:**

NoraSudduth.com

FunnelStore.com

FunnelKids.com

## About Ryann Sudduth

Ryann may just be starting middle school, but she's already on her way to success as she sets and achieves her goals. She earned her first-degree black belt in Taekwondo when she was 9 years old, and she's using what she's learned from her Mom and from Funnel Kids to help build marketing funnels for others and for her own business ideas.

Ryann is a budding artist who loves to sketch and design. She spends time sewing various projects for family, friends and her two dogs and cat. Ryann loves exploring and trying new things - from learning to ice skate to learning to play the flute. She's also been known to get completely lost in a good book.

# Skateboarding, Goodwill, and the 8-Letter Word that Would Change My Life Forever

## Kolby's Story

As the father of four children ages 18, 8, 6, and 2 years old, you'd think I'd have this parenting thing nailed. It's actually quite the opposite. From adolescence up unto almost adulthood, each one of my kids has taught me a very unique lesson. To be completely honest I am not sure any of us really have this parenting thing figured out. The parallel to business and being a father has many similarities.

Did you decide "hey I am going to have children." Or in many cases–maybe it wasn't a decision yet it was something you were thrust into.

In business did you choose the job you are in or did it fit the needs to pay your bills?

Did you choose to start a new company, or stumble into new opportunities to create a business?

What do you mean there is no "how to be a parent" manual??!!!

How much do I feed them?

How much sleep do they need?

What do I do when they cry?

When do I have children?

Should we have more than one?

Now think about business. If you have ever created a company, started a side hustle or have been around someone who has built a business – there are many similarities.

Where do I start?

What type of product or service do I create?

How do I get people's attention?

When do I hire people?

How do I market?

How in the hell do I sell the products or services?

Now think about this for a quick moment.

- You can go to school, you can take classes, you can apprentice to be better at building and learning how to build a business.

- As your children age you feed them, they sleep, they learn, they love, they grow. You haven't killed any of them yet and hopefully they all have made up until the point of you reading this chapter.

What is the main connection point between the two?

By doing the actual work, you learn the most valuable lessons that cannot be taught in any classroom or by reading any book.

You have to jump in, adapt, grow, produce, and provide.

Can you see the similarities between parenthood and business? They are both scary as hell and only work when you dive in and do the work.

I have to share something with you...

There is no secret to it.

You have to roll up your sleeves, get ready and dive on in.

When you commit and do the work, the lessons you learn across the board are the most valuable. Let me share an example with you.

As a father I wear many hats and hold many responsibilities. This is no different than how I am at the office or with my businesses.

With my children I am a father, provider, protector and partner to their mother.

My responsibilities in these rolls fall into a few buckets: love, patience, teaching, and mentorship. None of these are easy tasks and each one of them require effort. In order for me to be successful as a father I must be 100% present for it all to work.

For me, the hardest thing, and the thing I still struggle with, is the most important lesson to learn: patience.

Yeah patience...There I said it!

You know the word, yet do you really have a practice that allows you true patience in your relationships at the office, at home and even with yourself. Think about that for a moment.

The definition of patience is the capacity to accept or tolerate delay, trouble, or suffering without getting angry or upset. I almost get anxious and upset reading the definition of the word. The reason I know there is a valuable lesson in what my kids are teaching me, is rooted in how I have reacted when I was unwilling to accept the wisdom in the lesson.

Let me explain.

Every morning as we get the kids ready for school, the same challenge shows up. They are the same two tasks that have been and will always be at the core before leaving the house.

Eating and getting dressed.

Yes, they refuse to get dressed without what feels to be 4,000 reminders, up until I physically have to help them into their school clothes. The flip side of this is eating. Yeah, the kids who will devourer enough donuts to give Dunkin a run for the money, have zero want, will or desire to eat prior to leaving the house.

So, each morning this series of challenges becomes a true test of whit, skill, diversion and negotiation tactics similar to Liam Neeson in the action thriller *Taken*.

The next pieces are the importance into learning how not to do something.

The clock is now ticking as we have 10 minutes to get three kids fed, dressed and out the door. Two things can happen. I can choose to ignore the importance of patience and scream, yell and lose my shit. Believe me this happens more than it should.

Or I can choose to be patient in the process, add diligence and push through the emotions that cause us all grief.

In doing the latter – I feel better, the kids feel better, my wife feels better and the day is off to a great start. When I choose not to use patience the day starts off with a black cloud of emotion that is fair to no one involved. It is also a horrible way to start any day.

So, we have established that patience is important or we can choose to accept the opposite.

It is something that shows up in almost all aspects of communication, dealings and interactions I have daily. It's up to me if I choose to learn and execute the importance in the lesson.

Let me give you a few practical examples of how my children are teaching me the value in learning and executing patience.

## Noah's Story

Our six-year-old son, Noah, recently started skateboarding.

He absolutely loves it.

Every Tuesday we go to lessons and then we find ourselves at the skate park. If he learns how to drop in or basic push, each lesson and each day on the skateboard brings a new journey for him. He gets frustrated. He's not as good as he wants to be and each time he tries a new trick he gets that much more frustrated.

This acceptance and frustration is what keeps pushing Noah to expand on his current skill level.

Inherently, I want to jump down, grab his skateboard and show him what to do. At times, I've done that. Those are the times where he doesn't quite grasp the lesson and we become emotionally tangled into a tango or a dance between a father and a son. When I sit back and let him learn that lesson with very little direction and I take patience in watching him work through his own lessons and his own learning, he not only excels faster, he gets the benefits and the satisfaction of being able to complete something by himself and in his mind independently.

## The Lesson

One of the biggest lessons that I have learned through watching my young son, Noah, skateboard, learn a new trick, and seeing the tenacity it takes to succeed, is patience. To be successful in the marketplace, you must have patience. I can't tell you how many times I've had a great idea and thought, "This is the next big thing." Only to try to rush and push it to market and find that the market wasn't mature, the market wasn't ready, or the market did not reciprocate.

The market is the biggest equalizer. No matter how much you want to force feed your idea, your business principles, or your foundation down somebody's throat, if you're not there at the right time with the right offering, it's all for null.

# Sophie's Story

My eight-year-old daughter, Sophie Lane, recently approached me frantic with tears in her eyes and the slant of anxiety. Her annual Fun Run was quickly approaching. The annual Fun Run was the one time where parents and kids could raise money together to buy a series of things, toys, t-shirts, games, books. The kids waited all year to participate. This year, Sophie Lane had a specific goal in mind. It was not only a price tag, it was a series of prizes that she had her eyes set on. Sophie grabbed me, pulled her piggy bank out, dumped out the money and said, "Dad, can you help me count?"

We counted her money she had 17 dollars. The price tag for the goal she had in mind was 100 dollars. Immediately, she asked, "What chores can I do to go earn the balance?"

There are not enough chores I can assign an eight-year-old over a four-day period to allow her to earn $80 without me just giving her $80. We called her grandparents and they kindly donated $10 to the cause. That left Sophie with a $70 gap. She had seen me build an online course on teaching people the ins and outs of arbitrage (a.k.a., finding something to sell in your area to somebody else at a higher price) and asked if I could teach her how to sell books online like I had taught thousands of students already.

My eyes lit up as Sophie quickly grasped she could create her own wealth versus waiting for somebody else to give it to her. We jumped in the car and to the local Goodwill. I grabbed my phone that had an onboard scanner. Taking pictures of books, we went through hundreds of titles for over an hour and a half until we found books that were selling. We could buy at $1 and sell for up to $10 until Sophie could build the variance that she needed to cover the $70 gap.

Sophie brought a notebook and in one column, she wrote the cost of the book. In another column, she wrote the sales price of the book. In the third column, she wrote what her profit margins would be. She totaled up the columns and after spending her $12 dollars, she could make $95 dollars back.

Not only did she make the money she needed, she came home and found the independence on understanding that if she had a will, a want, a desire, and a drive, she could make money with her skillsets and talents, period.

## The Lesson

Growing up with divorced parents, I was forced at a young age to understand how to make money for myself. My family was constantly under the stress and pressure of living paycheck to paycheck. As I got older, I quickly understood that that was not the way I wanted to live. Learning how money was made, learning how to build a product or service, and learning how to solve problems has been absolutely key as I've grown older over the years.

Those are the skill sets that I've passed down to my children. It's key to raise problem solvers, not children who simply go through the process. By enabling them with the tools, the power of the Internet, and the power of positive intuition and positive reinforcement, our children will teach us more than we'll ever know.

So in these very different examples you can see the power of patience has been the linking factor. From learning new tricks on a skateboard to understanding the process of creating revenue streams – One thing holds the foundation together.

Patience.

In learning this key lesson I am a better father, husband & business owner. The lessons of parenthood are everywhere. It is up to us to identify, accept and engage in these lessons. There is one thing I know for sure; I learn something new from my beautiful children daily. They are my greatest blessing.

## About Kolby Kolibas

Kolby is a Business Owner, Entrepreneur, Author, Film Producer, Social Media Influencer, Global Marketing Expert, Husband & Father.

He spent over 15 years in corporate America as an executive running sales and marketing for companies such as IBM, Hewlett Packard, Microsoft, Dell and many others.

Kolby has advised, built and partnered with hundreds of startups that have generated millions of dollars in revenue over the past 10 years.

Helping entrepreneurs take ideas to revenue, Mr. Kolibas specializes in sales process, market penetration, social media and taking actions that produce results.

His belief system is that all people have a dream to do something that leaves an impact. His goal is to help as many people unplug from the "matrix" as possible to create a life they love.

Kolby is married to his amazing wife, Jennie, who supports his adventures. He is the father of four beautiful children. Ages 18, 8, 6 and 2 (aka The Intern).

Kolby has a love for martial arts, motorcycles, reading, art, tattoos, football, surfing, travel and spending time with his family.

**Facebook**
Facebook.com/ImKolbyKay

**Instagram**
Instagram.com/ImKolbyKay

**Twitter**
Twitter.com/ImKolbyKay

**LinkedIn**
LinkedIn.com/in/KolbyKolibas

**Websites**
TheHealthyPrimate.org
MeltdownEvent.com
RyanTechInc.net

**Book**
Why Your Life is Killing You - My Journey to Reducing Stress and Living to Tell About It

**Film**
Journey to the Sun Documentary

## About Noah Kolibas and Sophie Kolibas

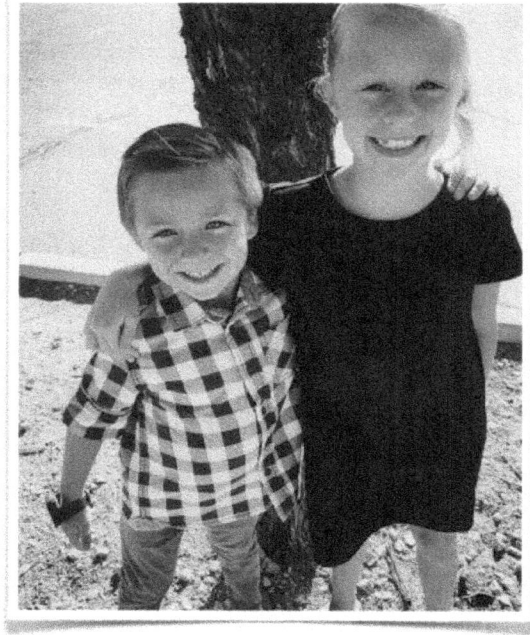

Noah is a passionate and loving six-year-old who loves to be outside. From his time at the skate park to playing with his siblings – Noah loves to stay active. He will never say this out loud, yet Noah is one of the sweetest human beings I have ever met. He has a heart as big as his arms can stretch and genuinely cares for all that he meets.

Sophie is our brain child. She picked up a love for school and the arts at a young age. This creative eight-year-old can be found drawing, painting or crafting her friends and family clay sculptures. She loves spending time with her family, soccer, and using her hands to build things. Just don't ask her to clean her room!

# Happy and Healthy

## Sara's Story

One of my favorite things about being an entrepreneur and working from home is the enormous amount of time I've been able to spend with my only son. He was born two months early (weighing only three pounds) and we both almost died to get him here. After being flown to the neonatal hospital in an emergency helicopter for his delivery, I was told not to have any more children.

I highly suspect that this impacted my desire to spend as many moments with him as possible which led to our decision to home school him as well. To make this dream come true, I quit my job as a traveling lead trainer for Dell, and I started working from home.

While I strategically designed my life to be there to educate my son, I ended up learning so much from him. Out of all the lessons he's taught me (and humbled me with) over the years, the most valuable one is that we can always choose to be happy.

While that may seem so simple, it has had a profound impact on my life and the lives that I touch. Whether I'm speaking on stage to hundreds, coaching private clients as a high-performance health strategist, or leading a group of clients building their business in the mastermind program that I run, this lesson comes up time and time again because in business and in life – there are always bumps in the road. While we can certainly strategically plan for these bumps and even choose routes to avoid some of these bumps, our ability to navigate life with a smile makes the ride much smoother and much more rewarding.

Even though my son was born so early and so small under such difficult circumstances, he's been happy since day one. On his first day on the football field at age five, he got his first tackle and came up with a huge grin that you could see shining through the front of his big, bulky helmet. That coach instantly nick-named him Smiley. Fast forward through years of sports to his starting day on the high school basketball team and that coach was still calling him that on the first day (with no idea that it had been his nickname for years.)

This is a boy who was born to a Mom that battled depression for years due to the trauma she endured (which included the loss of my son that I had before him) and a wheelchair-bound Dad who had both of his legs amputated above the knee from a car accident. Yet to this day as he nears the age of 18, he chooses to be happy every day of his life – no matter what circumstances he finds himself surrounded with.

My son could easily choose to focus on all the things his father can't do with him (especially in sports which are so important to him) since he has no legs to walk on, but instead, he consciously chooses to focus on the things they CAN do together.

My son could easily choose to focus on all the things his Mom couldn't do with him when she was suffering from severe PTSD symptoms, but instead, he consciously chooses to focus on the positive changes she made for both of them (and others) because of those experiences.

Not a day goes by in my business (and life) that I don't make a valiant effort to follow his courageous lead. One of the first things that I have clients and teams that I lead do is to practice a seven-day complaint fast. They go seven days without complaining (which is pretty much proven to have no value in life), and if they catch themselves complaining then they start over until they make it a week.

Once they adopt this attitude, they don't think the world is ending when they slip up on a food choice and have a setback on the scale. With these more powerful conscious thought patterns, they don't suffer from stress and anxiety when their first online marketing endeavor doesn't close as many deals as they'd anticipated. Instead, they choose to stay happy and hopeful while going back to the drawing board to create the results they desire...which then happen much more quickly and easily with this strategic frame of mind.

I love vulnerably sharing my personal experiences with my clients because it helps them choose a new, more empowering perspective that better serves them and further enables them to reach their goals – no matter what the setbacks and obstacles are. Even better yet, it helps them accomplish their dreams with a smile even when things don't work out exactly as they'd planned. That is where the magic of enjoying and making the most out of this short life can be found, and I'm eternally grateful that my son taught me this valuable lesson so that I could share it with so many others as well as reap the benefits of it for myself for the rest of my time in this great game of life.

## The Lesson

1. Happiness is a choice that's yours to make in business and life...in each moment...no matter what you're experiencing. It's a practice that becomes a habit that impacts every single day no matter what's going on around you. It's a powerful tool and once you learn to effectively use it, it becomes much easier to apply as needed.

2. Happiness is contagious. Once you master it and use it unabashedly, you can spread it to those who truly need it. You can be the light in someone's darkness and have a profound impact on the trajectory of the rest of their life. That's huge in my humble opinion.

3. Life is undoubtedly going to have lows. Things that we plan sometimes won't pan out. People we love will experience pain. We will experience loss. Choosing to be happy doesn't mean ignoring or suppressing the variety of other emotions we're gifted with...it means having a way out so that we don't get lost in them. It's a way to find a positive pivot so that we can enjoy the ups and downs of this quick roller coaster and genuinely enjoy and appreciate the amazing ride of life.

As my gift to you, get a free copy of my handbook "Nourish You Now: 33 Natural Health Practices You Can Start Today" at www.NourishYouNow.com.

## Cole's Story

For as long as I can remember, my Mom has taught me and her clients to put their health first.

This valuable lesson has allowed me to be at the top of my game throughout my sports and my academic affairs. It also kept me feeling good in my body and helped me to avoid ever getting sick.

Being healthy physically and mentally has allowed me to dedicate even more time and energy into accomplishing my goals both on and off the fields.

As a small child staying home with my Mom, I remember hearing her on the phone coaching clients. While I was glad to have her there all the time, it wasn't until I got older that I realized that the advice she was giving her clients was also sinking in with me.

If there's one thing she believes in, it's that we've only have one body right now so we should put it first to keep it performing well for us for as long as possible.

While I used to think that she was crazy making me take these supplements when none of my friends were doing it, now I realize that those practices helped keep me off prescription medications and helped me not miss any sports or school due to being sick.

I remember hating green smoothies for a long time but I'm glad she kept at it until it became a routine habit for me...I'm still not saying that I like them, but I like the way they make me feel.

I finally realized the full impact when I started high school and noticed what my peers were eating. I'd eat a healthy meal and have tons of energy while my friends would eat fast food and get sick and feel like crap. I definitely feel like that gives me a big competitive advantage both mentally and physically.

One moment that really stuck with me was when I was sleeping a lot over the summer when I was 15. Everyone said I was just being a teen but my mom taught me that just because something is "common" doesn't mean it's "normal." She refused to settle for that answer and she made me take the lab test that she gives her clients. The results revealed that I was off the charts deficient in Vitamin C, and one of the top symptoms of that is fatigue. After just a few days on her professional products, I was like a new person. I had way more energy and could think much more clearly. I hate to think that I almost went through an entire summer or longer simply accepting feeling that way.

I'm glad my mom helps people get healthy and I'm glad she stays healthy so that we can enjoy a long life together. I'm also glad that she teaches me and my family this so that I can also pass these valuable lessons down to my kids as well.

I can still remember the days where my Mom didn't feel well and I'm glad she made so many changes to correct that because she feels great all the time now which makes our time together much more enjoyable. I feel like there was my Mom before her health was her top priority and then there's my Mom now - it was a drastic change and I like my new Mom much better and I'm so happy for her.

All these lessons have added a small voice in my head that reminds me to look at what I can eat today to feel good for what I need to do. When I have sports, I think "what do I need to eat for this all-day track meet" versus "what do I need to eat for this late-night basketball game." For my studies, I think, "what do I need to eat tonight for this early morning test tomorrow" versus "what do I need to eat this morning to get through this long project today?"

These habits also alleviate the fear of me having to worry about major health issues later in life. One reason my mom went down this path is because both sides of our family have major health issues like diabetes, etc. so I feel like this plays a big factor in our drives to stay healthy and to help others in our family get healthy as well. She leads by example and now I do the same and you can see the impact it has on others which is very rewarding. I love our life together now, and I wouldn't have it any other way.

## The Lesson

1. The first major lesson that I learned from my mother about health was that eating the correct foods allow me to be the best I can be without feeling slow or tired from eating bad foods.

2. She also taught me that taking care of your body is one of the most important things that you can do to feel good in general plus feel good about yourself for making it a priority. It's a wonderful feeling knowing that you're taking care of your body and knowing that you're doing the best for yourself so that you can do your best in life.

3. The last most important lesson is that our bodies can heal quickly when we give them what they need. She makes sure we use nourishment before medications so that we don't have bad side effects or develop dependencies. I've never taken an antibiotic, so my gut health is super strong which makes the rest of me that much stronger.

# About Sara Flowers –
# DHP, CPNH, RYT, TRE

Sara has designed strategies and systems to sky-rocket and sustain health and growth for thousands of people both online and offline. A powerful and dynamic speaker, Sara has led training events at companies ranging from Dell to the Department of Justice as well as smaller Forbes 100 and Inc. 500 businesses.

With particular attention to stress and digestion, she creates custom health programs aimed at uncovering the root sources of problems that continue to sabotage most health goals. Sara uses a variety of non-invasive, cutting-edge tools to provide quick relief from health challenges related (but not limited) to stress, anxiety, sleep, digestion, allergies, skin issues, hormones, pain, discomfort, and much more.

Last, but not least, she's an audacious Author, patient Trainer, passionate Mentor, and proud Mom who loves family, friends, farmer's markets, nature, and yoga.

For more information and a complimentary copy of Sara's latest book, visit SaraFlowers.com.

**Facebook**
Facebook.com/Sara.Flowers.5817

## About Cole Flowers

Cole Flowers is a Senior in high school and is on the Varsity Basketball, Football, Golf, and Track teams. While he's been home-schooled his whole life, he plays sports at the local high school where he's extremely dedicated to contributing to these winning teams. To stay at the top of his game, he trains with former NBA basketball players as well as a US Olympic Gold Medalist coach. When he's not playing for the school teams, he plays on summer leagues. He's also starred in a professional theater production and been featured in a print ad. While that all keeps him super busy, he really enjoys time with family and loves playing video games with friends in the off season.

For more information, visit ColeFlowers.com.

# I Felt My Unborn Child Kick…
# and I Knew Something Was Wrong

## Mark's Story

My wife, Deena, placed my hand on her belly where she was carrying our child. I felt a slight movement—it was our unborn baby, kicking. Everything changed for me at that moment.

Until that moment, I'd been focused on the present: traveling the world, enjoying nice cars and large mansions and expensive yachts; spending time at the beach; eating at amazing restaurants. It was enjoyable and well-earned after a childhood of scarcity followed by years of hard work to grow my businesses.

But suddenly I realized that I was living only for the moment. I was working hard to reward myself *today*. Sure, I'd thought about the future and made sure that I was helping my family financially, and I put some money away into Self-Directed IRAs for my nieces… But that was it.

When I felt the baby kicking, it crystallized one of the most powerful lessons that my child has taught me (and continues to teach me daily).

I believe it is one of the most profound lessons anyone can learn in life.

I realized that I wasn't thinking beyond my own life. But when I felt the baby kick, I immediately thought of his lifetime. How would he grow up? How would he make his way in the world? What would he choose for a career? How would his children grow up? How would his children's children grow up?

In an instant, I saw many generations from now, each tracing their heritage back to me. And at that moment, I wondered how I could help each of them, and help the world at large, by the choices I make each day.

Until that moment, I was thinking too small. I realized I could make decisions today that have an impact for generations to come. I was focused on creating one ripple in a pond, not many ripples that would grow and grow and grow.

This is the lesson I realized at that moment: **We get one shot at life. Stop playing small-time and start building a legacy for the future.**

## The Lesson

Can I get real with you and speak very straightforwardly? Some folks might not like what I have to say, but I'll say it anyway: *Most people are playing WAY too small.*

Many entrepreneurs, for example, are focused on building businesses that survive for the first few years and then continue through their lifetimes. And then, as their business grows, they start to enjoy the well-deserved toys and experiences—like the stacks of cash, fancy cars, and high-end yachts.

Been there, done that. I traveled the world for seven years and experienced adventures on nearly every continent. Sure, it's fun to have the toys (and the admiration that goes with it), but this is all temporary. It doesn't last.

But you can have an impact that does last. Consider the life and legacy of George Vanderbilt. He didn't just want to build a nice home for his family; he envisioned something much larger—an estate that would be grand, self-sustaining, and last for generations. The Biltmore Estate was completed in 1895 and has been a legacy for more than 100 years... and will continue for years to come. There's a reason why we remember Vanderbilt: he didn't just focus on the rewards in his lifetime but created a legacy in the Vanderbilt Estate and in his many businesses that still impact us today. He saw beyond his own life, and he saw that he could impact others in the future.

I was born in very modest circumstances and discovered early in my life while watching episode after episode of *Lifestyles of the Rich and Famous* that you don't need to be BORN with a silver spoon in your mouth to be able to create the life you want to live and to leave a legacy behind. And when I felt the baby kicking in Deena's belly, the importance of the legacy became so clear.

It comes down to having a mindset of scarcity or a mindset of abundance. People with a scarcity mindset are worried that they will run out of money in their lifetime and they hold onto it and spend it carefully. People with an abundance mindset realize that they can use their money now to enjoy a good life today and also to have a greater impact for many years to come.

Most people focus their efforts on their own lifetime. But that is thinking too small. It's creating just one ripple in the pond. How can you create *many* ripples? How can you play bigger? How can you create a legacy that will go beyond your life and your children's lives, and stretch for many generations and impact your city, your country, and the world at large?

Most parents want to create a good life for their children. But you can do that and so much more, and have an impact on the lives of your children's children's children! I was put on this earth to do more than just live in a nice house and drive a fancy car. I was put on this earth to change the financial DNA of our family name.

Why were you put on this earth?

Stop thinking small.

What's the biggest thing that you think is possible for you to achieve in your life? Now consider: how can you expand that even more? What if you become the greatest in the country, or even the greatest in the world, at the very thing that you are doing now? What would you need to do to accomplish that? Who would you need to help you? What reward would it give you? What impact (legacy) would you be able to have on others— family, friends, your community, the less fortunate—if you expanded your vision to be even greater than you'd ever thought possible?

Most people think small and live small, never realizing they can have more in life. With Mark III's inspiration, I am continuing to grow my life and my business to help other people have more— I'm building a legacy of my own that will last for generations, and I'm helping other people create their legacies as well.

As an entrepreneur, what I've realized is: if I want to leave this legacy, I must create a business foundation by building a company that outlasts me. Think Apple. Even though Steve Jobs is gone, Apple continues to thrive. A key part is hiring great people. I see lots of entrepreneurs try to be everything and do everything. We all work hard but who is working smart? Many are building a great business today, but as soon as they're gone, the business shuts down. We take a lot of the responsibility and work on our shoulders. But at what point do we hire talent to create a company that continues?

In my own life, I am building businesses that will serve my family for generations to come. (And not just mine and my wife's families, but also the "family" of people who are my employees.) With this inspiration, I'm more motivated than ever to continue building one of the largest turn-key real estate investing firm in the world.

Through my company, American Wealth Builders, we are having an impact on other people. My team and I are helping our clients build legacies of their own through investing in cash-flowing, game-changing real estate inside or outside their IRAs and 401(k)s so they can create a legacy for generations to benefit.

I'm leaving a legacy with my eight bestselling books and the people I coach and mentor, showing other real estate investors how I've built my business and what they can do to create an empire of their own.

When I felt Mark III kick, I realized that even though I had been working toward building a legacy for myself, I was still playing small.

My child and your children represent the next generation. We owe it to ourselves and to them to stop working only for the present. We need to shake off that small thinking, to step up, to think larger, to dream grander visions, and to create bigger things in our lifetimes so that the legacy we leave behind will impact our children and many generations to come.

**Recommended Action Steps and Things to Think About**

- Think about the business you are building now. What happens to it when you are gone? What if you could grow and expand it so it continues for generations to come?

- If money weren't a factor, what would you do with your time and wealth to have an impact on others? How would you serve? (Now think about how you can do that now, and in the future, through your business.)

- If you passed away today, what would you leave behind? How do you want to be remembered a year from now? What would you need to do differently to be remembered 100 years from now? What can you do, starting right now, to contribute enough to the world so that people will still be talking about you a hundred years from now?

## I Hope My Son NEVER Learns to Walk

By Mark Evans DM (about lessons learned from his two-year-old son)

*Mark III is too young to write his own chapter, so I'm writing it on his behalf to share what I hope to teach him about life.*

I grew up in a small town in Ohio, the son of hardworking blue collar parents. They loved their family and worked hard to give me and my sisters all the advantages they could. But the truth is, they struggled to make ends meet and felt limited to what they could achieve in life.

Likewise, my teachers looked at my poor grades in school and thought I wouldn't amount to much, and they placed limits on me as well. "Academics is not Marks' strong point," they'd say. "Maybe find a career where you don't have to go to college." Or, "The best you can hope for is a low-paying job," they told me.

I had two paths to choose from. I could have gone down the path that everyone said I was destined to take. Life wouldn't have been fun, but it would have been a default "regular" life, with a family and a minimum wage job, and the rest of my life set out for me. That would have been the easy choice (and the truth is, that's the choice that many people make in life: to choose the path of least resistance).

But there was another path—it was the harder path. A path of potential risk and failure but also a path of bigger rewards.

Think of it like the difference between swimming downstream or upstream. If you swim downstream, you go where the current takes you. It seems easier but the external environment directs where you go—how fast and how far. But if you swim upstream, it takes a lot of work and effort and struggle (and sometimes failure), but you go as far as you want. YOU determine your outcome. Those are the two choices I had in life and, in fact, they are the two choices anyone has in life.

Most people default to the easiest one. Downstream. The path that is determined by others.

As an entrepreneur, you are someone who chooses the potentially harder path and swims against the current. This against-the-current life takes a special quality that must be cultivated.

And that leads me to the lesson I want to teach my son. That he can do anything he wants, and he can swim upstream in life. But to do that, he needs one special quality: **Fortitude**.

## The Lesson

Times have sure changed since I was a kid in Ohio. In some ways, it's easier than ever to create your own life (thanks to how the Internet has connected us to each other and created more opportunities); but in other ways, it's harder than ever to create your own path in life.

The reason why it's harder is because we're not rewarding those who put in the effort to create their own way. These people are being punished and taxed and derided.

Today we're coddling children to get a participation medal; we're rewarding those who don't pull up their own bootstraps to work hard to swim upstream. We are rewarding those who are carried by the current downstream and punishing those with fortitude.

I don't need to tell you that being an entrepreneur is hard work and we don't get a participation medal. You either win or lose. Both are okay but it takes fortitude to win, and it takes fortitude to pick yourself up from a loss and keep going.

Parents aren't helping! They say to their children, "You can do anything you want to do." BUT after graduating from high school they tell their children that the next step is college to "figure out what you want to do in life." Parents end up creating a path for their children that forces those children to give up many of the best years of their lives in pursuit of a default "downstream" life.

Meanwhile, parents (and society at large) are holding their children's hands well into adulthood and bailing them out of difficult circumstances rather than letting those children discover their own inner resolve.

If my son wants to go to college, he's more than welcome to. But he doesn't have to. I will tell him that he can do anything he wants in life, and then I will teach him to have fortitude to go and get it.

He's not going to get a car from me when he turns 16. He's not going to get an allowance from me for making his bed or cleaning his room. I would rather equip my son with a priceless mindset to face the world. Just because your family is wealthy doesn't mean you will be.

We as entrepreneurs make life look easy from the outside in but I don't want my child to think it is easy and expect it to be easy. We weaken it by giving them everything and making it easy and just solving everything for them with our connections or money.

I want him to develop the fortitude to step up when the going gets tough. It's a tough world out there and no one is going to hand out a trophy for just showing up.

So, one example of how I'm teaching Mark III fortitude is: he and I wake up together every morning and he joins me in my office!

He may not understand what I'm doing but he sees me working early in the morning, reviewing spreadsheets and dealing with challenges and working opportunities. He knows that I work hard to earn my rewards. And, no matter what he chooses to do in life, I want him to emulate that hard work and to strengthen that "swim-upstream" muscle of fortitude.

In those early days in Ohio, there were temptations for me to accept the life that had been seemingly "assigned" to me. But I knew I wanted to grow beyond that rural life, and since I didn't have the academic skills that others had, I needed something else to help me achieve my goals. What I did have was fortitude, and that helped me to get off the path I was born into and to create the path I wanted to go down, a path that has helped me become an 8-time bestselling author, and the founder and CEO of one of the largest turn-key real estate investing companies in the world.

And what applied to me getting out of that small-time life also applies to every other entrepreneur in the world... and it's one of the most important lessons I hope my son learns.

Want to know why entrepreneurs struggle and ultimately fail in their efforts to grow a thriving business? Sure, it's easy to blame circumstances like the economy. It's always easier to blame some other factor. But there's really one key reason why most business struggle and fail: it's because most entrepreneurs lack fortitude.

When I look around the world today I see a world of virtually unlimited possibilities and opportunities. But so many people are being coddled and handed participation trophies. We are creating a world of people who aren't equipped to handle challenges they will encounter.

How many entrepreneurs read *The 4-Hour Work Week* and tried starting a business in just four hours a week? How many of those entrepreneurs gave up as soon as they realized that *The 4-Hour Work Week* is a myth, and it actually requires more like ninety five hours a week? The sooner you realize that the true secret to achieving your goals in your business is fortitude, not the easy path, the sooner you will achieve your goals.

Like many of the entrepreneurs reading this book, I built a business and wanted to hit my goals right from day one but that's not possible. It takes constant focus and patience to push through the daily challenges. As a result, other businesses that started around the same time as mine collapsed while mine pushed forward step by step.

My business, American Wealth Builders, has grown because of my unyielding fortitude to keep building.

I want Mark III to know that he can do ANYTHING he wants, to enjoy financial freedom and time freedom each day, without having to delay that gratification for his golden years. I want to show him that there are amazing opportunities all around, if he will only look with optimism and then pursue those opportunities with fortitude.

Even though he's just two years old, I demonstrate these lessons to my son every day. I demonstrate it now, and will teach him when he gets older to harness information and technology to help other people.

I will show him that opportunities abound if he will simply pick something and then focus on it patiently, and that life can be enjoyed right now as you take advantage of every exciting opportunity each day. That said, I also want him to know that it's not all unicorns and rainbows in life. Every entrepreneur is going to get smacked around by hardship. Therefore, you must be focused and work toward your dreams.

At the end of Mark III's life, I want him to look back without an ounce of regret, to say that he truly lived every day to the best of his ability to pursue the opportunities that arose.

Mark, my son, read this daily: *Don't let anyone tell you that you can't accomplish amazing things in life. You have the keys within you to grab hold of every opportunity—focus and patience.*

## Recommended Action Steps and Things to Think About

- There are many opportunities in the world and you probably see a lot of them. But what would happen if you focused just on one until it grew?

- How big do you want to grow (and what if you could grow even bigger than that)?

- What obstacles have stopped you in the past, and how might fortitude have helped you overcome them?

- What obstacles exist right now that seem to prevent you from achieving your biggest dreams?

- What can you do to remind yourself periodically (hourly, daily, weekly, monthly, yearly—as often as is necessary) to dig deep and revive your fortitude?

- What are some specific ways that you can teach fortitude to your children?

## About Mark Evans DM

No one thought Mark Evans would graduate from high school. But Mark had different plans for his life. He did his first real estate deals before he turned 19 and that changed everything. Today, he's called "The Deal Maker" (The DM) and "The Digital Nomad" (The DN) because he owns a massive real estate empire, which he runs while traveling the world. The DM is also an 8-time bestselling author; the creator of multiple innovative, cutting-edge real estate software; he's the host one of the popular podcast shows, TheRealEstatePowerHour.com; he's a go-to real estate investing coach to the gurus.

He has a straight-talk, no-BS approach to sharing everything he knows about real estate, business, and building multiple streams of passive income from anywhere in the world. And his legion of loyal students know that he teaches the very strategies that he, himself, uses day-in and day-out to do his deals.

Mark Evans DM,DN also gives back. All money earned from the sale of his books is donated to charitable foundations, and Mark regularly gives away fully refinished and furnished houses to homeless veterans.

Mark is also the self-proclaimed Greatest Father in The World.

To his friends, his students, and even to those who didn't think he'd graduate from high school, The DM says: "I've only just started... You should see what I've got planned next!"

**Facebook**
Facebook.com/MarkEvansDM

**Instagram**
Instagram.com/MarkEvansDM

**LinkedIn**
LinkedIn.com/in/Mark-Evans-DM-4994228

## About Mark Evans III

Mark Evans III is just two years old and he's already taking the world by storm and walking in his father's footsteps when it comes to doing deals!

Mark Evans III is one of the youngest Self-Directed IRA holders in the world (earning 70.5% ROI annually inside his IRA!) He's the owner of multiple investment properties, and he's even the bank for other people's investments.

And since he's as handsome as his father, he's also a model for American Wealth Builders.

Very shortly, he'll be a #1 bestselling author at the ripe old age of two.

Most importantly, he's the owner of His Destiny and will grow up to do whatever he wants.

**Facebook**
Facebook.com/MarkEvansDMjr

**Instagram**
Instagram.com/MarkEvansDMjr

KiddieRothira.com – Free report on how a 1.5-year-old is getting 70.5% Return on his Roth IRA

Want to learn how to create double digit returns without all the headaches and market up and downs?

Get the FREE Report at www.AmericanWealthBuilders.com

Or if you want to see how to turn your Retirement account into a cash flow machine get over to www.KiddieRothira.com and get the FREE case study showing you step by step how this can be done without any early withdraw taxes.

# Survival Unlocked What My Heart Actually Wanted

*"Commitment is what transforms a promise into reality."*
*–Abraham Lincoln*

## Renée's Story

I didn't realize it growing up, but I've always been an entrepreneur. Perhaps you can relate. I'd bet if you look back, you'll find all sorts of wondrous clues to help answer your 'what was I born to do' mystery.

I love how entrepreneurs tend to view problems; it's an uncommon perspective. We look beyond the surface. When others perceive misfortune, our mind speaks, "Opportunity." We're able to detect beauty amongst the ashes and awaken imagination. Ideas consume our thoughts as we work to identify the root of tangible issues. We're convinced we'll help make the world a better place once we unearth the solution and we indeed do just that.

From the lemonade and snow cone stands at the end of my street, to helping my grandfather paint his wooden creations for sale at his Cape Cod shop, to playing store with childhood friends and cherished stuffed animals; I wanted to learn about, and participate in, business. I was often coming up with creative ways to make a buck and practicing entrepreneurship without understanding what I was actually up to.

Call it chance, call it fate, call it God; My pursuit of business wasn't intentional.

In 1998, I entered the selling arena at the age of 18. By 20, I was earning more income than most adults. After hustling my way into upper sales management, I decided against college. I spent the next 14 years in a slew of commission-based jobs as an employee with a desperate longing to be my own boss; a craving that was nothing more than a starry dream until a trial would have it become otherwise.

I gave birth to a precious baby girl.

"Trial?" You may question.

The moment I saw the positive pregnancy test result in my hand through fear-filled tears, I knew. I knew this journey was going to be difficult due to complex circumstances. It was far from ideal, and I had substantial reason to be scared.

But. I also knew I had no other choice and something inside me whispered, "This is the beginning of the end." Every sacrifice, every tear, every ounce of invincible pain, every fight against— what felt like—the world and every misunderstood moment I've endured to be a mother, has been worth it.

There's an immense purpose for our suffering. If we'll allow it; Our affliction gives us a greater capacity to capture deep appreciation, to learn selfless love and to pursue an unrepeatable calling despite fear.

Despite popular belief, the life we experience is not a matter of circumstance, rather it is a matter of how we choose to respond to our circumstances.

Being a mother is one of my dearest accomplishments.

While examining how my role as a parent impacted my business, I was reminded of the extreme tests I've confronted and the bona fide love residing in my heart today because of the messy road.

The war of art has become my beautiful castles in the sky.

Life is full of inevitable peaks and valleys; both are equally good. I share the grunge for the one in pursuit of prominence; We must be prepared to address the cluttered muck tucked neatly under the rug of our souls throughout the trek. You will find no shiny object here. Serious grit is mandatory when your passion is to take your last breath at peace, knowing your life ended with an exceptional conclusion.

The miracle is found at the end of the struggle for the one who chooses to persevere.

We all face tribulations. Some more so than others. Still, hardship is hardship. It's what we know as our intimate heartache–not meant to be understood by everyone–in conjunction with our prolonged highway of twists, turns and brokenness.

Have you ever felt as though you were living, yet not alive?

I've learned that light shines even in the darkness. Try as it may, darkness can never extinguish it for the one who keeps their eyes fixated upon the light, even when it seems hardly within sight.

The battle is what transformed my character and improved the overall quality of my life.

While reflecting for this book, I discovered hard truths:

Prior to my daughter, I had never wholly committed to anything. I got bored quick; a result of not understanding why I was living. I retired from endeavors too soon, even the things I was really good at. Therefore, I couldn't undergo the change essential of anyone hoping to arrive at individual greatness.

Prior to my daughter, I had unconventional dreams that caused my eyes to twinkle and my stomach to flutter, but were nothing more than an enjoyable notion.

Prior to my daughter, I was paralyzed by doubt, fear, and insecurity.

These facts played a quiet role in keeping me from crucial growth.

We all have dreams, yet few achieve them.

Les Brown said, "The graveyard is the richest place on earth because it is there you will find all the hopes and dreams that were never fulfilled."

How sorrowful it is to never attain our hopes and dreams.

Raising my daughter as a single mother has taught me many things about what's most important. It's made me a better woman. And it's positioned me to achieve qualities of substance: courage, strength, and ability that I never knew existed within me.

Before my daughter, I had an aspiration to become an entrepreneur. The aspiration didn't become a reality until after her.

As I pondered the essence of my success, one word came to mind.

Commitment.

Commitment is an instance of being obligated or emotionally impelled to a cause.

Prior to my daughter, I thought I was committed. But now that I've walked the walk, I can see the difference between saying we're committed and behaving committed.

Genuine commitment never gives up. Therefore, it never fails. It's disciplined and consistent. When we've agreed to commit with sincerity, we feel obligated to see it to the finish line.

We tend to celebrate the success of others without consideration of the fight. Yet without the conscious daily fight, success cannot be sustained.

*"Burn the ships." – Cortes*

In 1519 Hernan Cortes, accompanied by 500 men and 11 ships, landed in Mexico. Upon arrival, he commanded his men to burn the ships. Why? Because once the ships were ruined, their only hope was to defeat the enemy. They had one option to stay alive; commit wholeheartedly to conquering Mexico.

The only stage guaranteed is the present.

There are a few questions we should mull over before drafting our plan.

What is the one thing you aspire to gain now?

For Cortes, it was to claim Mexico for Spain. For me, it was to become an extraordinary example to my daughter.

Who is your enemy?

For Cortes, it was Mexico. For me, it was myself.

How much do you want to fulfill your dreams?

For Cortes and I, it was enough to lead to the defeat of our rivals.

Commitment is achieved when there is no other option. The men traveling with Cortes felt compelled to conquer Mexico. I felt compelled to be a remarkable mother and offer my daughter the deep-seated desires of my heart. I retain an intense conviction to be the woman I've always needed. But what pushed me in the direction of real devotion and continues to do so, was my strong belief of who I needed to become to change my legacy, along with an insatiable yearning to give my daughter a life without limits.

The commitment to conquer led Cortes and his men to claim Mexico.

The commitment to my daughter led me to take a leap of faith. Taking a leap of faith led me to commitment to my business. Commitment to my business led me to success.

To make our dreams reality, we must be sold out to commitment.

However, commitment alone isn't enough to brave our foes.

I grappled with and puzzled over doubt, fear, and insecurity. I felt too flawed for the fire in my chest to go from wish to existence.

Destructive words haunted my heart and mind.

I can't.

Who am I?

It's been done before.

Why me?

It's impossible.

What if I fail?

I'm not qualified.

What will people think?

Etc.

Immersed in commitment bigger than myself, my ego took this massive blow and wanted to retreat. When we become dead set on the victory of unleashing our inner genius, some ugly giant appears to destroy us. In this single-handed battle against darkness, I uncovered how flawed I truly am. Faster than I could blink, my unpleasant opponents doubt, fear, and insecurity grew louder due to my perceived imperfections.

Our flaws–the hurts, habits, and weaknesses we all contain– cannot be ignored during this 'becoming of our best self' quest. Because we're all flawed. This wild adventure to mastery exposes our true character so that we can become the champion we're destined to be.

So, how does one stand up to resistance disguised as doubt, fear, and insecurity amongst flaws?

## The Lesson

I made the commitment. I located the splendor in my shortcomings and embraced what makes me...me; my strengths and weaknesses, my good and bad, my pretty and ugly. And I implemented these five keys to help me persist on the less traveled path toward success, regardless of my adversaries.

**FLAWD**

The 5 Keys to Staying Committed

1. [F]aith: We must have faith

2. [L]ove: We must love

3. [A]ccountability: We must be held accountable

4. [W]hy: We must know our why

5. [D]ecide: We must make the decision

## F – FAITH

We must have faith.

> *"Faith is to believe what you do not see; the reward of this faith is to see what you believe." –Saint Augustine*

When a new movie comes out, they don't market the entire film. If they did, no one would pay to watch it. Instead, they release a trailer meant to pique interest. God does the same. What he wants to do in and through us is beyond our understanding. Therefore, like the marketing of a new movie, he reveals just enough for us to take action.

With faith as tiny as a mustard seed, you can move a mountain. Release yourself of the need to know it all. You could never comprehend the outcome of what seems impossible. Allow yourself to follow the unknown with trust in a higher power.

Follow the small still voice within that whispers the way you should go; Day by day, hour by hour and minute by minute. Appreciate one moment at a time.

As I look back I'm astounded by what I've completed; the places I've gone, the person I've become and the people I've encountered. Had I rejected the small still voice guiding me, I would have missed it. There are many miracles to be amazed by when we let go and respond to our calling with an open mind.

What is the small still voice within you saying?

## L – LOVE

We must love.

> *"I've learned that people will forget what you said, people will forget what you did, but people will never forget how you made them feel."* –Maya Angelou

Love is our greatest strength.

Be the giver. Be an example of true selflessness—willing to love even when it's difficult and especially when you don't want to—going above and beyond to help others get what they want.

To help myself become a person who loves fiercely, I meditate on this unmatchable definition of how to love:

> *"Love is patient, love is kind. It does not envy, it does not boast, it is not proud. It does not dishonor others, it is not self-seeking, it is not easily angered, it keeps no record of wrongs. Love does not delight in evil but rejoices with the truth. It always protects, always trusts, always hopes, always perseveres."* –1 Corinthians 13:4-7

These words teach us easier-said-than-done type of love. If we love others this way, we'll one day wake up with everything we want. We search for solutions when love has always been, and will always be, the answer to everything.

I'm unafraid to take radical action to spark feelings of love, connection and significance in others. My actions confirm my words. The only outcome I hope for is that I play some role in helping others get whatever it is they want.

How will you love others?

## A – ACCOUNTABILITY

We must be held accountable.

> *"It is not only what we do, but also what we do not do for which we are accountable."* –Moliere

We're all responsible for using the gifts, influence, resources, and talents we've been given for the greater good.

You possess something no one else has. You've been given such so that you can make a difference with it.

It's been said, "When the student is ready, the teacher will appear." We're in a constant state of revolving teacher-student relationships. Each position is necessary and of equal importance. There are people unbeknownst to you, waiting for you to show up as your whole self; ready, willing and able to multiply enormous change so their purpose may prevail. Although our intention is to bless others, we find ourselves blessed. As we do, we further become.

If you don't spend time doing such, you risk dying with regret while robbing the world of this breathtaking mission you're supposed to complete. You have a higher purpose, and it is your obligation to live it. For you, for mankind, and for God.

I consider the cost of having to answer for squandering my gifts greater than the cost of the troubles I'll face while putting them into practice. I carry a strong conviction that my life is not about me, rather it's about the oppressed and those who I can motivate toward stepping up to serving others with a heart of compassion. For me, it is God, myself, a handful of trusted people and a set of high expectations that hold me accountable.

You have a calling to execute and people to lead toward success.

How will you be held accountable for what you do, and also what you do not do?

## W – WHY

We must know our why.

*"Success is fulfilling your soul's purpose." –Jack Canfield*

You will never reach unclear goals. The more specific our goal is, the more potency it has. This includes the who, what, where, when, why and how.

Look back and listen to what your life is telling you.

This is your purpose on the planet and your reason for being. Knowing our why keeps us moving forward in the face of adversity. Our why is our motivation. If we don't know our why, we will give up when the going gets tough.

We tend to give up on ourselves before we give up on others.

Your why is larger than you.

My why is my faith, my family and those I believe I'm here to help. The fear of failing my why exceeds my emotions. Therefore, it helps me to remain committed, even when it's burdensome, and I may not want to.

Make time to identify your why.

Who and what other than yourself drives you?

## D – DECIDE

We must make the decision.

> *"It is in your moments of decision that your destiny is shaped."* –Tony Robbins

You must plant your flag with the belief there's only one option—conquer. There is no plan B or plan C. There is only plan A.

Decide with a non-negotiable attitude, whatever the cost.

This is you saying, "No matter what comes my way, I'm not giving up."

In a race everyone runs, but only one runner gets the prize. Run to win.

I've made execution my only option. Too often we justify backup plans, but what do these other plans imply? If we have a backup plan, we've chosen it. Backup plans are prone to be easy and are rarely the authentic hope in our heart.

The awesome power is in one option. What is your one option?

Having faith, loving others, being held accountable, knowing your why, and making the decision is the secret sauce for staying committed to your purpose so that you can come face to face with the success you've been created for.

Flaws that once stopped me, now empower me.

It's never too late.

Commit to the pursuit of your dreams with all your heart and never give up.

# Leana Marie's Story

## The Simple Truth About Standing for Your Destiny When It's Not Popular

One thing I've learned from my mother is that we shouldn't do something just because everyone else is doing it. Instead, we should be and do what we believe is right. As a kid, you want to be liked so this isn't always easy.

Even though I'm young, I've already experienced having to stand up for myself many times. As we grow up, there's a lot of pressure to do things you might not feel are good.

This happened recently over my best friend's house.

I was invited to her sister's birthday party. I didn't know many of the kids going, but I was still excited. It was a big sleepover with 25 girls, including me.

As soon as I arrived, I put on my bathing suit to go swimming and picked out where I wanted to sleep. I chose to stay with my best friend and six other girls.

The day was awesome!

We swam, ate, laughed and had my favorite cake and ice cream.

But at night I was faced with an uncomfortable situation; Several girls came to our room and said they were going to do the 3 A.M. Challenge.

I'll explain, in case you don't know what it is.

This challenge has gone viral. People on YouTube claim 3 a.m. is the devil's hour, and Siri will take over your phone to haunt you. There's a bunch of videos with titles like, "Do Not Talk to Siri at 3 AM Creepy Challenge!"

A parent found out and put an end to it.

I was relieved, but it caused some drama and the birthday girl was upset.

We all went to our spots for bed shortly after.

Around 1 a.m. three of the girls came into our room and said, "We're going to do the 3 A.M. Challenge, but we want to do it here."

There was no easy escape this time since the adults were sleeping. My new friend Emily, my best friend and I all told them no because we didn't want anything to do with evil.

The girls offered a snide reply, "This isn't church, why are you always talking about God?" Even though they go to church.

Emily said, "You can't just go to church and be like I love God, then leave expecting him to be there while you completely forget about him."

After that, they went away.

While this was happening, I asked myself a question, "What would my mom do?"

She teaches me a lot about life. I took my friends hands and suggested prayer. We each prayed twice. Once we finished, we all felt this huge weight lifted off our shoulders and were able to sleep peacefully.

I told my mom the story as soon as we got in the car.

We talked about how it isn't easy to stand up for what you believe is good when people are against you, but we'll be glad we did in the end. It's powerful to understand and apply this concept to every area of our lives.

## The Lesson

Written by Renée Jean and Leana Marie

Here are four things I've learned by standing up for what I believe:

### 1. We have all been created on purpose for a purpose

God gives everyone exclusive talents to be used for the greater good. We have this innate tendency to compare ourselves to others and subconsciously metamorphose into them. There's certainly value in learning from someone else. However, if we're not careful, we can lose ourselves in the process.

We're not meant to be like anyone else.

Everyone has been created on purpose for a purpose, but it's one of a kind. We're meant to grow throughout our lives. As we do, we become—as we become, we're able to accomplish what we're destined for. No one else can carry this assignment to fruition for us. The technique we use to hit the bull's-eye of our purpose will look diverse, yet the ultimate end game is identical. We're all called to love God wholeheartedly, and to love others without expectation.

We get hung up on legacy, but as Maya Angelou said, "You have no idea what your legacy will be." It will be every life we've touched so we should be sure to do everything with love.

## 2. We must know what we believe and why

Dave Ramsey said, "Live like no one else, so you can live like no one else."

Have you made honest time to consider what you believe in and why?

Many people don't fully understand why they believe what they believe. Rather, for several justifiable reasons, they follow someone else. This is a dangerous way to live.

It's impossible to remain standing when faced with adversity if we're not confident about our opinions. Because if we don't stand for something, we'll lay down our lives for anything. We're in a war zone. There is good and bad all around us. It's good to fight, but too many people are fighting the wrong way for the wrong things.

There's a small still voice strategically planted within each of us. It's the hardest voice of all to hear and ironically, it's also the most important voice of all to hear. This voice whispers without boundaries. It guides us to our truth, tells us the way to go and leads us to love.

## 3. We need to surround ourselves with like-minded people

We were created to be part of a diverse community full of color, age, race, and wonder. Two are better than one, because together they can work more effectively.

Time alone has merit, but we're not meant to linger there long. Culture is gently creating isolation and addiction—Social media establishes this false sense of connection. With every like, comment and friend added we plunge into a silent, deadly trap; we mistakenly believe we're 'connected' when in reality, we're pushing away what matters most of all.

We must understand true purpose and power lies within real relationships, with real people, who believe in and are willing to stand with one another through good and bad. The deep connection between a small tribe bears hidden energy that's capable of moving mountains, defeating giants and conquering impossibilities.

## 4.  We should live in a way that is without regret

How will you live and how will you be remembered?

There are two dates we're all guaranteed: the day we're born, and the day we die. It isn't easy to consider mortality, but oh how persuasive it is. Ignoring the fact that we'll die offers the illusion of time we don't have, whereas acknowledging it, offers the appreciation required to maximize the time we do have.

One of the top reasons why people fail is because of their fear of people. Fear is usually false evidence appearing real so why do we allow others to dictate our future?

We will either fight each day to be who we truly are, or we will spend our lives being who others want us to be. Our character grows when we stand firm in the fire. Through difficult situations, such as pressure from others, we become stronger when we do not waver.

Fear is a liar.

We're afraid to be who we are because we know there are people who will stand against us. Therefore, we cower. We live to please these same people who will never be satisfied. No matter who you are or what you do, there will always be people who exist to fight your calling. The opposite of fear is love. We can choose what we'll spend our life putting our faith in; fear or the reason we're alive.

There are people who will not only like us but who will support and encourage us. These same people are waiting for us to unapologetically show up as our unabridged self. By doing so, we instigate others to become who they were created to become and accomplish what they were created to accomplish. I can't think of a more magnificent snowball effect.

As parents and children, we have the power to change our legacy and our world for the better as we take a stand together for the good of who we are and what we believe.

## About Renée Jean

Renée Jean is a Real Estate Investor, Author, Coach and Speaker striving to create change and cause miracles in the marketplace through messages of faith, hope and love. The main purpose of all she does is to help people crazy enough to think they can change the world, do just that. She silently suffered from chronic depression from the time she was 10 until 35 years old, despite her efforts, continued success and many blessings. God's unexpected deliverance at an unlikely place secured her deep conviction in miracles. She believes the greatest problem we face today is the mass of people suffering from feelings of being unloved and unwanted, and that it's our responsibility to use all God has freely given for a higher purpose. Her mission is to tell the world the truth about limitless love, eternal life and infinite freedom. She lives to serve God and humans wholeheartedly by using her gifts, influence, resources and talents for the greater good. She currently resides in Massachusetts.

If you've found your path crossing with Renée's and you're craving an out of the ordinary transformation, she can help you get there.

Go to www.iamreneejean.com and sign up to receive a copy of her latest eBook for free! Change doesn't occur by chance. It takes courage, commitment and community. The principles contained in her blueprint are the exact strategies Renée used to overcome hopeless giants to experience massive breakthrough so that she could become the woman she was destined to become.

**Website**
IAmReneeJean.com

**Facebook**
Facebook.com/IAmReneeJean

**Instagram**
Instagram.com/IAmReneeJean

## About Leana Marie

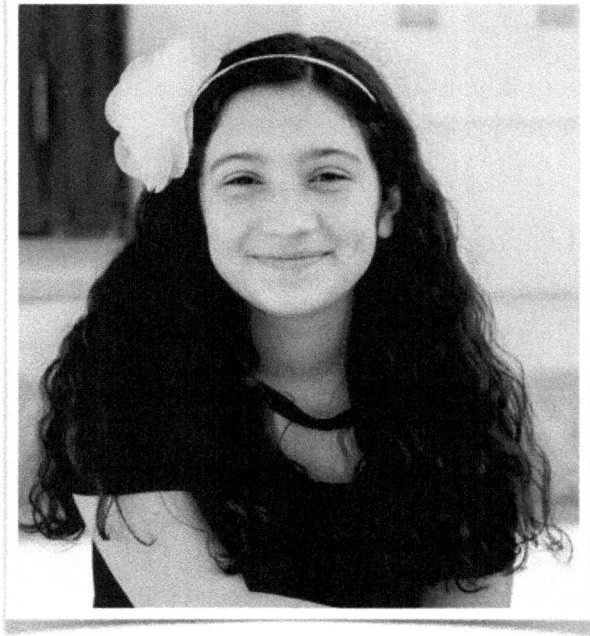

Leana, the daughter of Renée, is 12 years old and just started the 7th grade. She enjoys Girl Scouts, music, drawing, writing, creating something out of nothing, making people laugh and spending time with friends. She has a voice that will give you chills and takes lessons weekly to strengthen it, although she seems to unintentionally sing the loudest when it's the least practical. She has a passion for all things horses. She's a natural with these glorious creatures. When it comes to horses, she will find a way to be with them, even if it means offering a helping hand around the barn. She dreams without limitations, and her childlike faith is catchy. She's played an active role in her mother's line of work since she was five years old and aspires to establish her very own business.

# Building a Legacy

## Raul's Story

My wife and I got married in our early twenties and, instead of having kids right away we focused on building our business. The longer we waited, the more we got comfortable with the idea of not having kids. It was to the point that I was doubting if we were going to have one. Every time my wife would bring kids to the conversation, I would give her excuses on why our life was perfect the way it was. It turns out I was afraid to have kids because I feared I wasn't going to be a good father. I was so focused on conquering the world that I didn't think I'd ever have time for kids. After seven years of marriage, we finally decided to grow our family.

Everything changed the day my son was born. I remember it like it was yesterday. For twelve hours straight, my wife labored to bring him into this world. She endured body-splitting pain as she pushed, but my son refused to come out. After many hours that seemed like days had passed, the doctors noticed my son's position was incorrect and that the umbilical cord was wrapped around his tiny head. My wife's pain continued with an emergency C-section.

I witnessed the entire procedure. I had a front row seat as the surgeon sliced through my wife's abdomen to help my son. When he finally arrived, I could tell he was going to be a fighter. As I held him in my arms, I realized this little man was going to need me to up my game. I couldn't play the game the same way anymore.

I said a prayer to God and thanked him for giving me a beautiful baby boy. I swore in that moment to protect him, guide him, and give him strength whenever he needed me. Nothing else in the world mattered except being the best father for my son. He was my everything.

As tears poured down my face, the doctor took my son away to examine him. I had just witnessed a miracle, but the moment was changed when the doctor told me my son would need to spend the next seven days in an incubator. He had jaundice, a condition that caused his skin and eyes to yellow because his liver couldn't process things effectively.

Just a few moments before, I had promised to protect him. Had I already let him down?

I felt like a failure. Seeing him in the incubator scared me and broke my heart. Each passing day blended into the next and seemed to last an eternity.

The day he finally got to go home was the best day ever. I thought the worst of it was over. I was wrong. Shortly after we got home, we noticed he couldn't breathe at night. We took him to the emergency room where doctors said he had developed asthma.

Each night, I had to put a respirator on his mouth and nose so he could improve his breathing. He was so small that the respirator mask nearly covered his entire face.

Throughout all this, I noticed one thing. My son never stopped smiling. He smiled in the incubator. The same smile graced his perfect face while he used the respirator and never left as he grew stronger and bigger. It never changed. His smile lights up a room.

He's eleven years old now, and we've had many adventures together. His smile has endured throughout them all, both good and bad. Knowing all we've been through, I asked him why he smiles so much. He said he feels loved and that keeps him smiling.

## The Lesson

I believe the pain I experienced during the early years with my son is a metaphor for my life's purpose. As I tried to conquer the world of business, I put off things. I realized I put things off in business because I wasn't ready. I told myself I needed more money and education before I could start my business.

Once passion gives birth to purpose, life changes. You wonder why you waited so long to get started. Just as with my son, a business is fragile in the beginning and requires lots of nurturing to grow and expand.

I've realized one thing about myself when it comes to business. I tend to start another business before I let the other one develop enough strength to stand on its own. I've learned a different approach by watching my son grow.

It takes time.

Growth doesn't happen overnight. Every stage has its gifts. If you rush through the phase you're in, you'll miss the opportunity to embrace the next phase.

Every moment with my kids is precious just as every moment with my business is precious. They grow as a result of the love I give them. My son grew up healthy because he received unconditional love from his family. Our attention to him made him stronger. The same is true with my business - it grows because I love what I do. I understand every business has its phases and cycles and my job as an entrepreneur is to fall in love with the process, not the destination.

Having my son helped me see I can't control everything that happens. I may not be able to protect him from everything that may come his way as he becomes a young adult. As long as I teach him to smile through both happiness and adversity, I am certain he will find a way to overcome.

## Alejandro's Story

What were you doing at the age of five? When I was five, I went to school just like every other kid. On Fridays, my dad would pick me up at exactly 3:00 pm. He would pull up the car right in front of the school with his loud, pumping music and the teacher would call my name, "Raul!" But I already knew my dad was there because I could hear his music. I'd quickly get into the car, and my dad would say, "We have to go to the office first, then we can go home." At first, it was just a couple times, but after two weeks he started taking me to his office every single Friday. It became like my "job," too. When my dad took out his keys and opened the door to the office, I looked around and noticed everyone was always so focused on their work.

I would sit down in a chair and look outside while he worked. I could see the clear blue sky and watched the leaves change from yellow to orange and red. My Dad thought I didn't pay much attention to what he was saying, but as I looked outside my brain was absorbing all the knowledge my dad shared with his clients. I didn't even know it at the time, but I was taking it all in. I remember having a special chair to sit in when I went to "work." That was always my thinking place. I loved that chair because it was in my dad's office. After a while, it became my chair.

My dad taught me more and more about real estate sales, and eventually, I went to open houses with him. I thought (when I was seven) that I wouldn't use any of the experience I was getting.

I remember my first 100-Day challenge. It was go-time. I had to apply what I had learned from my dad so I could earn my first iPhone. The challenge required saying power statements to push me out of my comfort zone. This process was my daily ritual. I was dedicated to doing this every single day. I would wake up in the morning, brush my teeth, and make my bed. After that, I would go downstairs to my living room, and no matter who was there, I would make my power statements. I was sure to use the same tone of voice that I would if I were alone. I did that for one hundred days. It seemed like a hard thing to do but, after a while, it was just part of my morning routine. With my Dad's encouragement, I completed my challenge and earned my very first iPhone.

The day I finally got my hands on it, my heart was pounding hard. My head was exploding with excitement and anxiety as I waited for the day I'd get my iPhone. When we went to the store to I couldn't focus on anything but the iPhone. We picked up the iPhone and as soon as we walked out of the store I knew that it was perfect for me. I wanted to open that package more than anything in the world.

I was so excited to tell my whole family. It was the best feeling because was proud of myself. I earned that iPhone with my own efforts. When we got home, I bolted out of the car and went to tell the whole family. When I was done, my dad pulled me aside and told me that I would be responsible for my phone bill. At first I thought he was kidding. "I'm just a kid," I thought, but he was serious. When he spoke with me later that night, we decided that I should raise money for my new bill by doing videos. We came up with this idea because I always made little videos with my dad. He would say what he needed to say then I would chime in and add my thoughts to his content.

We agreed that I would do my videos for my dad in my free time. A one-minute video was worth five dollars. I was always excited when my dad would pay me for my work at the end of the week. At first, I wouldn't look at the camera, but my dad would push me. I was too shy to do these videos in front of people because I didn't like that they would watch me. But I had to keep doing it, and soon I got comfortable. I knew if I put in the work I would get money in return. Now, I do it because I know people watch it. Since I didn't have a platform to post on at the time, I would give my dad the videos to post on Facebook. After doing this for some time, it was finally payday.

On payday, my dad handed me $15.00 in cash before he passed around checks to all his employees. I didn't understand what the piece of paper meant, or why everyone seemed to be so happy. I finally asked one of the employees to see theirs, "May I see that for a minute?" When I saw the number on that check, I jumped back and ran in circles! After a few minutes, I walked right into my dad's office and told him I needed a raise. Of course, he was shocked, but he heard me out and we had a conversation. He told me that if I wanted to make more money, then I needed to prove that I was worth it. "What are you going to bring to the table to earn this raise?"

If you want to make more money, then you must work harder. For me, the solution was to learn to edit my own videos. Not only was it a valuable skill to learn, but it gave me more control of the final outcome. Also, my dad didn't need to spend his time or pay someone else to edit them for me. This meant he could pay me more for the videos I put together. My dad encouraged me to use iMovie like he did, and I figured it out as I went. No one taught me how to do the things I was doing. Yes, my dad gave me tips, but at the end of the day, I had to figure out all the complicated things on my own. I played with the editing tools for audio, and background, etc. for my videos and eventually understood how they worked.

I wasn't afraid to try new things anymore, and I was getting used to doing these types of videos. After that, I was paid ten dollars for every video, and every time I made one, it got easier. This meant each video took less time with practice, and I could create more content which led to bigger, better paydays. I eventually opened a savings account and put all the extra money in there. My dad saw my potential in all the content I created and decided it was time I managed my own platform to share them. I was very young, so he supervised my Facebook account, but I've been posting videos on it ever since. I was eight going on nine, but more importantly - I was hustling.

## The Lesson

After all that, I am still building my brand and doing more projects with my dad, if not on my own. When I first started out, I didn't know how to do much of anything, but I learned new skills throughout the process. My dad taught me many things, like how to get out of my comfort zone, but it was up to me to continuously push myself to do more and to do better.

Through my journey, I was constantly challenged. I pushed myself to talk to more people, and thus developed impressive social skills. Every time my dad pushed me, I made a lame excuse and tried to avoid these exercises. I thought that the little exercises he gave me were a pointless waste of time. One day my dad asked me if I wanted to see why social skills were so important. I was curious, so I went along with it. Next thing you know, I was at a Tony Robbins "Unleash the Power Within (UPW)" speaking event.

While at the event, my dad made it a point to prove to me how helpful and valuable social skills could be. By the end of the day, my dad had at least 40 different business cards, all with contact information to people who now knew who he was. After that experience, I understood what my dad was talking about, and used my new-found skills at similar events to make life-long connections.

Over the years, I have met extraordinary people who have given me great advice. The first was Caleb Maddix, the founder of Summa Success. When I saw how intelligent he was, I immediately took out my iPhone and got him to join me in a two-minute video. I remember that day because he saw how confident I was. I also had the opportunity to spend some time with Gary Vaynerchuk, another brilliant entrepreneur. He is not only a

Judge on "Planet of the Apps" (a show about pitching apps), but he also runs a company called Vayner X which is the parent to several other entities and partnerships. I have also attended several Tony Robbins events - those are always highly motivating. The very first one I went to was about challenging the way your mind thinks. He had us walk on fire to get his point across. That was an experience I will never forget.

My father shared his wealth of knowledge and experience with me so I could push myself like he always did. Together we took chances and explored new opportunities. Now, I understand the true meaning of the word "potential," and my only goal is never to stop having goals. The minute I stopped making excuses and started taking chances, I began to grow in more ways than I could count. Imagine if I didn't do the exercises my dad showed me, would I even be writing this?

## About Raul Villacis

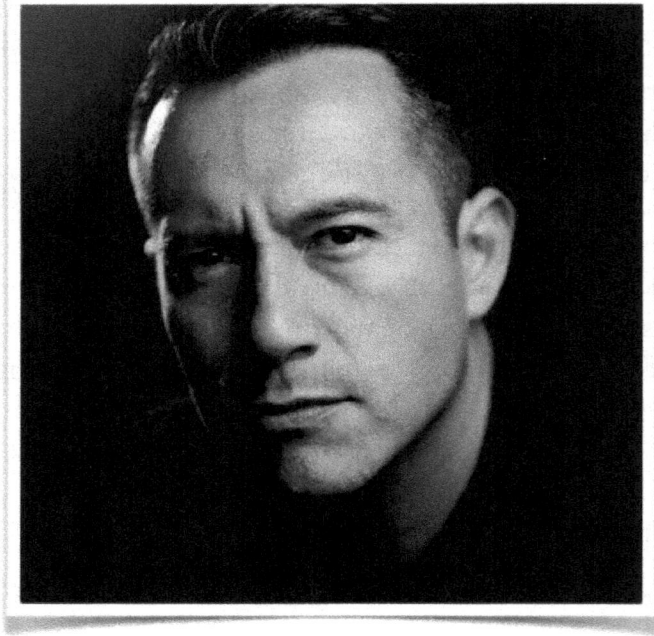

Raul Villacis is an entrepreneur, investor, and mentor. He is the founder The Next Level Experience – an organization designed to help successful entrepreneurs and CEOs find clarity and achieve balance in their personal and professional lives. The system that he teaches is called "The EDGE" and the boot camp style mastermind gives men the opportunity to re-discover the edge they once had. His programs have been sold out and he is currently working on expanding his events to Latin America. In addition, he owns a real estate firm and a media company that produces content for distribution. He began his journey as an entrepreneur at the age of 23 when he started his own real estate company. By the time he was 30, his real estate company had become the largest Latino-owned real estate investment firm in

Connecticut. Servicing major financial institutions and hedge funds his company found a way to tap into a niche market.

He is a contributing writer for Entrepreneur Magazine as well as Forbes. In addition to his work with The Next Level Experience and other businesses, he's passionate about helping the next generation of entrepreneurs find their message. Together with his son, they have spoken on many stages to inspire parents and kids to take the risk and find their purpose. You can find out more about him at www.RaulVillacis.com

**Facebook**
Facebook.com/RaulTheEDGE

**Twitter**
Twitter.com/RaulTheEDGE

**Instagram**
Instagram.com/RaulTheEDGE

**YouTube**
YouTube.com/RaulVillacis

**LinkedIn**
LinkedIn.com/in/RaulVillacis

## About Alejandro Villacis

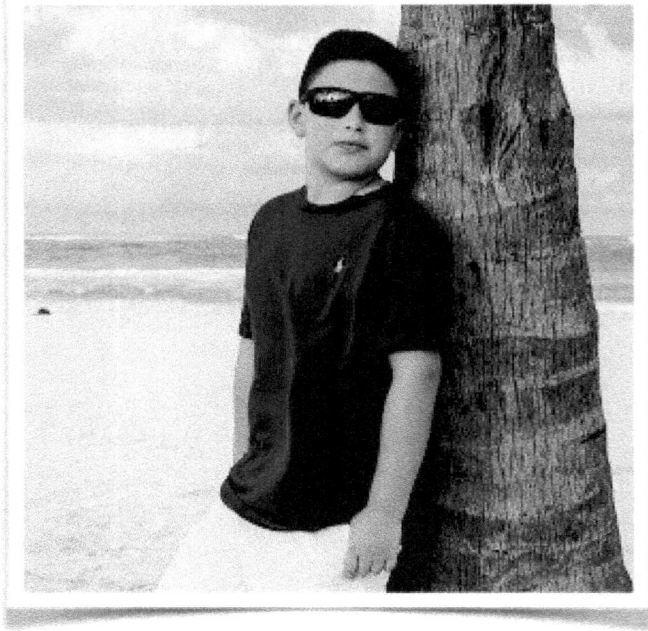

Alejandro Villacis is a young entrepreneur who loves sharing his message of becoming an entrepreneur. He has sharpened his negotiation skills at his father's real estate business since he was five-years-old and has built upon that foundation through speaking at many engagements about the power of social media.

His brand, "A.LL I.N K.I.D" gives him the platform to share his journey with other kids and to teach them how to become entrepreneurs themselves. He has reached hundreds of thousands of social media viewers with his powerful and energetic videos.

He is passionate about inspiring kids of any age and background. He believes every dream is worth following and nurturing so you can realize your life's purpose. Don't wait until you're too old to get started!

He has been featured in videos with Gary Vaynerchuk and on the Entrepreneur Network. He is currently working on a reality TV show that shows kids the ins and outs of the real estate business.

**YouTube**

YouTube.com/channel/UCYkvuUZ-4R3xuyd2hHO7PJA

**Facebook**

Facebook.com/KidInfluence

**Instagram**

Instagram.com/KidInfluence

# The Power of Presence and Patience

## Brandon's Story

I've been an entrepreneur for about a decade now. For the majority of this time, I was constantly rushing around, juggling 100 things at a time and running on fumes at the end of the day as I was edging closer and closer to burn out. I think we can all relate to this. It's the hustle and grind mentality that although has some value at times, is not an ideal method of practice for daily living as a healthy and successful entrepreneur.

Being a single father changed this for me. I feel deeply blessed to be a father. And I've always felt that I was doing a good job carving out time for my daughter and I to connect and do things together. Not realizing I was becoming consumed by work and business, I had a very eye-opening conversation one day with my daughter. She said to me, "Daddy, I wish you would not speak over me as much and not be working on your phone as much." She was six years old at the time, and she told me that I have a habit of speaking over her and that I'm on my phone a lot.

Talk about a wake-up moment. It hit me hard when she said this. I couldn't believe I had become "that dad" that was distracted by technology and work and not being more present with my daughter.

It forced me to slow down and be more present and more patient.

Present.

Patient.

These were the two biggest lessons my daughter gave me about my business. You see, to actually show up as a father to her I needed to dial in my ability to be present and patient. This practice, although originally started so I could be a better dad, started to spill over into my business and work life as an entrepreneur.

I started approaching my day differently. I started meditating before opening my laptop or hoping on my phone. I started connecting more with my team and business partners. I started creating more space between meetings and work-related responsibilities. I am much more productive with my time and less busy now, simply by mindfully practicing the art of presence and patience.

This experience of having more presence and more patience dramatically impacted my business and allowed me to actually do more in less time because I was focused, clear, and powerfully efficient. Instead of late nights grinding away with too much caffeine and too little sleep, I was now accomplishing more productive work in less time while growing the business and having more fun along the way.

Plus, and my favorite part of all of this, I was able to spend more time with my daughter—more present, connected, and enjoyable time together where I was not distracted with work and not being a reactive dad.

The best way to apply this practice to your business is by creating a clear daily routine that allows for a few powerful practices that will clear your mind and help you create some space. Meditating for about 20 minutes is a non-negotiable for me, as well as time blocking my day and never working more than 90 minutes at a time without stopping to move and change my environment briefly. I also create "black out times" with technology now. I don't check email or social media for the first two hours after waking up and turn my phone on airplane mode when I pick my daughter up from school, and I wait until she goes to bed before turning it back on.

## The Lesson

I've built my business and work life so that I can mostly operate from anywhere in the world with my phone and my laptop.

Because of this, my daughter and I can travel quite a bit and spend more free time together. I share my daily practices and habits with her, and she now practices a few of them with me.

It doesn't matter where we are or what we're doing, I always practice my core daily habits. My daughter watches my every move. She sees me journal and read and meditate and exercise. She watches me record video messages of appreciation and send the messages to friends and family. Slowly, she started asking questions about some of these habits and activities I was doing. She started showing curiosity and wonder.

I was invited to give a talk to her first-grade class at school about the benefits of mindfulness and meditation. Isla later told me it was "cool" that I came to her school and taught her friends about this stuff. That's when she really became interested in learning more about the work I do and how I manage my business and my life.

It started with meditation. She saw me doing it and would ask to do it with me. She once asked, "Daddy, I don't really know how to do it, but can I sit and meditate with you?"

At first, we would just sit together with our eyes closed for about 60 seconds while she giggled and squirmed around and then once the timer went off she would let out this big burst of laughter that she had been holding in.

Eventually, she started asking to use my Muse Headband. This was the game-changer for her. With the Muse, she can sit for a five-minute meditation and see her actual brain activity data after. She will tell me, "Daddy, when I meditate I feel more calm and peaceful. I like doing it."

She has even gone on to use the breathing exercises she sees me use when she is nervous or really excited and trying to calm down. She said, "I know why you meditate and breathe deeply now daddy. It helps your mind work better and you stay calm and happy."

She'll say to me, "Daddy, I want to be an antra-pwenew-ar when I grow up so I can be just like you."

I smile and look her right in the eyes and say, "Isla Jo, you can be whatever you wanna be when you grow up, so long as it makes you happy."

# About Brandon James Duncan

Brandon James Duncan is a serial entrepreneur: restaurant owner, speaker, lifestyle coach and creator of the lifestyle performance brand, Rare Inc., Brandon is a single father and ultra endurance athlete that lives life in pursuit of discovering who he really can become. He's completed multiple Ironman triathlons, he's trained with Navy Seals, and he has a deep passion and desire for teaching others how to create their most rewarding life. He now lives in Portland Oregon with his daughter and their dog Cooper.

Want to learn more about Brandon and how you can work with him to start creating your most rewarding life? Send him an email at brandon@rarebreed.life

**Facebook**

Facebook.com/Brandon.J.Duncan.3

**Instagram**

Instagram.com/BJamesDuncan

**Website**

RareBreed.life

## About Isla Jo Duncan

Isla Jo is a second grader with a passion for music, swimming art and more. She loves animals, hiking, and indoor skydiving. She has several pets that she loves dearly, and says she wants to be an entrepreneur when she grows up. She was born in Alabama and now lives in Portland Oregon.

# Become A Single Mom and a Millionaire Simultaneously in Three Simple Steps

## Maria's Story

1. Get divorced right after having a baby

2. Lose everything and have no money or job

3. Start from scratch, figure it out, and make 7 figures

Ok, so those aren't simple steps, but the formula sounds great, doesn't it? The entrepreneur in me had to find a way to spin it with a clever marketing line and formula. Wink.

Yes, humor and sarcasm get me through life and writing isn't my favorite thing...so, if you don't mind, I'm going to write as if we are sitting together and chatting. I'm usually a pretty direct – cut to the chase kinda talker, so grab a cup o joe and get cozy, I'm going to share a bit of my journey and hope it may help someone trying to raise a child, build a biz, or both.

That was me 10 years ago when I got divorced. I had been married for 17 years (started very young), was a good employee in the corporate world, and pretty successful for my age at the time too. I didn't live life on my terms then, and as a result, all aspects of my life, including my health, suffered greatly. I was the good church wife. I stayed in a marriage and tolerated certain "activities" for many years before I finally drew a line in the sand... let's just say if you knew me then and know me now - you wouldn't have recognized me at all.

My divorce was devastating to me, I had no idea how or what I was going to do by myself with an 18-month-old, no family around, and no money. I left my job several years earlier to be a stay-at-home mom because I DID NOT want someone else raising my daughter! After throwing my adult tantrums, I decided this was do or die for me, and I knew a few things for sure:

1.  This is my chance to completely reinvent my life – to do something unprecedented.

2.  I will not put my kid in day care, therefore I'm not going back to a job.

3.  I will prevail...no matter what.

Those were strong driving forces for me.

Fast forward to now – when I look back on what I accomplished and what I was up against, when I stop to think and feel it, all I can think is that I would never want to do that again, and I don't know how I made it through. I just kept focused on what was next-constantly. However, when I really dive deep and remember the thoughts I had at the time, I was actually crystal clear on some very important visions and tactics. I didn't voice them at the time because I didn't feel others would believe me, and I preferred to win the race and prove it instead.

After hearing my story-- in interviews, when I get off stages, or when I'm at biz meetings--I often get asked how I accomplished what I did. So, I'm going to share a few of the most important tidbits that I hope may help others who really want the independence and freedom that can come with being an entrepreneur, even if they feel the odds are against them.

Before I share those tidbits, I want to point out one of the most important aspects of my story is that the majority of the skills or methods I used in parenting were universal in business too – so anything you read here is interchangeable.

First, I was extremely intentional with how I did everything – I even named all my biz names starting with the word intentional! I was not going to let any area of my life slip through the cracks because of my circumstances. I knew exactly the lifestyle I wanted to live, and I was willing to sacrifice six years to make it happen – which I did, six years to the exact month I committed to. That required thinking with the end in mind, and reverse engineering it from that.

I wanted to be able to work from anywhere with just a phone, have high profit and low overhead, homeschool my kid and travel the world with her, make seven figures and only work when I wanted to.

That didn't come easy, a lot of people sell the simple solution, which we all know is B.S. I was a full-time pre-med student paying my own way while also attending a distinguished homeopathic school at the same time; AND I started an acute care practice at the same time I was building my online system (which is a big, big system, the one that earned the 7 figures), and I was taking care of my daughter practically full time by myself... that meant VERY LITTLE SLEEP!

I pushed myself hard but going back to school at age 36 terrified me. I had failed school my entire life and was a high school dropout. I now know that it had nothing to do with academic ability, and had everything to do with circumstances. Even though I got my G.E.D. one week after dropping out, I lived my life thinking I was too stupid to go to college. I assumed I would have to plow through life the hard-grind way that my mom and dad had taught me. I was no stranger to hard work--I had been working three jobs since I moved out at age 15. So, when I nervously enrolled in college. I was determined to get a 4.0... which I did.

I was committed to working smarter, not just harder. This is why I'm so thankful for the gift of my divorce – it disrupted those old patterns of thinking! I felt like I got a second chance at life and I was going to build it on my terms this time.

The most important thing I could ever share with anyone who wants a lifestyle like the one I created is this: You have to have a fire under your ass – something that makes you go all in. For me at the time, my ex and I weren't amicable, and he was just waiting for me to crash and burn so that he could have more or full custody – he made a significant amount of money and knew I was hanging by a thread. Thinking of anyone taking my baby from me was all I needed as motivation. Hopefully, you don't need the same kind of fire under your ass as I did, but if you imagine something similar that has high stakes for you...I promise you will find a way to create your life around your vision.

My daughter trumped everything in my life – I was a very intentional parent. I wanted to be the example for any life lesson I wanted her to learn. I raised her using the Montessori methods and teachings because I feel it is so in alignment with entrepreneurial thinking: independence, life skills, curiosity, a love for learning in general. I wanted her to learn the skills I felt were most important to get through life--skills like being resilient, adaptable, persistent, relentless, flexible and kind. Over the years, she has sat in many audiences watching me on stage, she even got to be on a TV series with me.

Kids are a natural feedback loop – I don't need to preach to her or simply tell her what to do...I look at the results of what she is or isn't doing, and it tells me if I'm missing the mark, and then I realign my strategy to hit the target. She has taught me so much along the way (if you don't get offended by their feedback or take it personally or do the parent guilt game, you can learn a lot – little secret sauce☺).

One of my favorite feedback moments where I got to see a glimpse of the culmination of all she has witnessed from me come to life, was when I was speaking at a smaller mastermind event. I spent quite a bit of time on stage, and she was sitting at a round table with all adults in the back of the room interacting with them like she was a pro. About 4 hours later I saw her moving quickly in and out of the room on her phone (she was only ten!), I went to one of my team members who traveled with us and said where is she and what is she doing??  He said, "I don't know, she just asked me if I was willing to help her make some business cards," and I said, "Yes" (she was already being resourceful like I taught her)!

I went to find her out in the hallway and saw her pacing the floors on the phone looking like a Wall Street hustler making a deal. I said, "What is going on!?"  She said, mom I'm busy, I started my business today, and I'm getting clear with Celine (her BFF at the time) on the terms and if she wants to do this with me or not. She told me she had created her logo already, got someone to make her biz cards, knew how many hours she wanted to work, how much she wanted to earn and how much she needed to charge to make it all happen. She then showed me her marketing plan, logo, and all those numbers...and honestly, here all this time I didn't think she was listening or paying attention. Boy was I proven wrong – and blown away by what she created, it was amazing!

Not only did I engross her around all aspects of my work, but I would share my strategies with her along the way, too. At live events, I explained how important a good personality and being authentic is, and I would tell her to watch how I interact with people. I truly believe my success was fueled by my personality, integrity and by being unapologetically authentically myself. So, I would explain all those things and then demonstrate it for her...repetition is a foundational Montessori learning method – it works. She has a killer personality, is quite fearless, and sports a sense of humor that adults find funny--and at 12 years old, she's unusually confident!

Those traits are partially just who she is and partially a result of the intentional things I did to foster them. I'm an unconventional thinker, and I teach her things that aren't the norm – like I want her to learn more about how to generate money than how to save it. When we are in another country, I show her how I would generate money if I lost my biz and had to start over. Once you know the art of making money, you can replicate it anywhere, doing anything. I also wanted her to see that making money can be easy, you can do work around what you enjoy, and traveling the world is easy and doable.

I don't spoil her, nor do I make her grind or harp on her about chores, etc., because the kids I've seen who are the happiest and most successful had a less stressful childhood in general. I volunteered with junior high school students for 20 years, so I've analyzed hundreds of scenarios and saw many common themes/outcomes, and this was one of them.

I also believe that self-esteem is built by self-accomplishment, so I let her figure a lot out on her own. She also learns to fail forward as a result – which I believe is critical to learn if you want to get a biz off the ground and have it be successful. She may be a bit cocky, but what I do know is that it is a lot harder to rebuild self-esteem when you don't start off with it (how many adults spend most of their life trying to rebuild it?!), and I know that life can be brutal and will help humble and balance her out naturally. I'd rather her start with her cup full than empty.

I homeschool her now at age 12, and she gets to learn real history traveling the world with me, she drives herself hard in gymnastics and has a ton of great friends at her homeschool "school" that is like a group of Jr. High entrepreneurs. It is amazing to witness!

You truly can create life and biz on your own terms, be clear what you want to create, put a fire under your ass, and don't stop until your vision comes to fruition! One of my mentors said something that really stuck with me when I was freaking out after my divorce and how I was going to survive. He said, "Hold everything loosely," as he held his hands open, but together. I found that to be the thing I reminded myself of the most. You really do have to learn to ride the waves of life, be flexible and adaptable; it is as brutal as the ocean, but just as magnificent and limitless. Enjoy the ride!

## Riana's Story – The Biz Kid

I want to be a homeopathic traveling veterinarian. I learned how to start my own business from my mom. She taught me that you should start with the people around you, like your neighbors and your friends. So, I started with making my own business cards and marketing plan. The business I am creating is called Pawtastic Dog Walking. I started it because I LOVE animals and I want to spend more time with them. I've seen a lot of animals when I have traveled that need help with their health. It is an awesome experience for me because I'm starting at such a young age and I feel like this will make me a better person when I am older.

One thing I have learned from watching my mom in business is how she treats people, and how important it is to treat people well. We are always working to improve ourselves.

I went to a church camp recently, and that camp has taught me so much about God, myself, and forgiveness. When I was there the pastor talked about a girl named Kelsy; she was having a rough time cause her dad was cheating on her mom and left them to be with that girl. Kelsy joined a life group, and they taught her about forgiveness. She learned how to forgive and she called her father and said, "Dad, I forgive you for leaving us, I forgive you for hurting mom, and I forgive you for hurting our family," and her dad was speechless. So, they hung up and her dad called again, and he said (crying), "Kelsy, I'm so sorry I left you and mom and the family, I'm so sorry." I learned from her story how to forgive and I have learned how to Trust God and how to talk to him when I am feeling sad and alone. I feel like I have a connection with Kelsy from her sharing her story with us.

I want to spread that love with animals and people. Specifically, animals that have been rejected by their owners and left to die, or people that have given up hope and had no other options than to live on the street. I hope to use my business to help prevent these problems one day.

My mom helps humans and animals heal, I want to only work with animals, so I study the natural remedies she uses so I can become an expert.

## The Lesson

There are a few important subjects I have learned some specific things from watching my mom run her business and getting to be involved on many levels that I know will help me become a successful entrepreneur too:

### Money
I've learned how to earn money. You can't expect to have money given to you. I've learned that I can make money doing the things that I love if I create a lot of value for my customers and solve their problems. Money is everywhere; people just don't tap into it.

### Resourceful
I've learned how to be resourceful. I can think really fast of how to fix something or find the right person to help.

### Sales
I've learned how to do sales from my mom and from all the events I've attended where other experts teach sales skills. I can make the value of the product just what I need and what the customers would buy and how to communicate it effectively.

## Request

I've learned the power of request. People are afraid to ask for what they want because they don't want to hear a no. If they don't ask they will never get what they want and if they get a no it's not the end of the world.

## Negotiate

I've learned how to negotiate. I learned how to get what I want by not just asking but suggesting things that I want. Like when asked if I could have ice cream and my mom said no, I asked again if I could have ice cream after dinner she said no, I asked again if I could have ice cream, but I would take probiotics after and she said yes.

## Homeschool

I love being homeschooled because you can have a snack when you're hungry. You can go to the bathroom when you want. I have a homeschool community where I have a lot of friends who also have free time to do things others can't during school days. I have a lot of freedom. They let me be creative. They make it so you like to learn. The best part is spending time with my mom and getting to travel the world with her. We just got back from Galapagos Islands, and I studied all the animals on the island for almost a year before going, it was one of my favorite trips so far, and I know there are so many more to come!

## Self-Care

Probably the most important thing my mom has taught me. I eat right, compete in gymnastics and take good care of my mind and body. I even get massages weekly to keep my muscles healthy. I see a lot of sick animals and hear about a lot of sick people just being around my mom's work, and I don't ever want to be sick. I used to play soccer, and so many of the kids had allergies or had to take breaks to use their inhalers or couldn't play because they were sick. As my mom says, "we don't do sick". Prevention is always smarter, and I'm so thankful I've learned how to take care of myself starting young.

I'm grateful for my life and all the experiences I get to create and be a part of. I love building life how we (with my mom) want it to be; I feel empowered for my future.

# About Maria Whalen

As the pioneer of true individual health freedom, Maria Whalen is transforming alternative and western medicine worldwide.

After battling back from near death and healing herself completely of so-called "incurable" diseases, Maria created her groundbreaking *Invincible Wellness System*.

Maria reveals how to become your own doctor and gain complete control of your own health so you never become sick again. The *Invincible Wellness System* frees you from today's healthcare system, giving you complete and total independence.

She is the figure that industry leaders, entrepreneurs, and titans of business turn to for invincible health.

If health freedom, liberation, and independence are important to you and you want to protect your greatest asset, YOU, then you must experience the powerful presentation by author, international speaker and leader of the Self Sufficiency Movement, Maria Whalen.

**Learn More at:**

IntentionalNetwork.com

IWSbook.com/mrmh

## About Riana Whalen

Riana Whalen is an energetic 12-year-old. Her hobby is gymnastics. She loves animals, and she travels the world with her mom! She lives in Orange County C.A., and she likes to do crafts. She has two step brothers.

# What Do You Want?
# Act as if it is Certain.

## Marshall's Story

I did the unusual thing of waiting to find the right wife before I started having kids. I was married twice before I met my one true wife. My babies are fairly young relative to me. I'm 55, and the babies are six, four, and two.

One of the things I think that has been extremely good for me in having waited so long is I believe that I'm much wiser than I would have been if I had started having kids when I was in my early 20s. The patience factor is one of the most important elements. I can truly hear my children and listen to my sons and my daughter before I make a decision, rather than just reacting to the circumstance that's going on. I make sure that I take the time to ask, "Hey, what happened?"

If they're crying, I first ask, "Are you hurt?" If they're in physical pain, they have a legitimate reason to be crying and screaming. Once they've told me what's going on, I simply tell them,

"Use your words." If they're upset and they're screaming and they're not making any sense, that phrase, use your words, is a very powerful phrase to use.

Oftentimes there'll be a circumstance where my kids won't want to do something, and getting them to do something might mean I need to offer a buffet. I have to say, "Okay, would you do it for this reason? Would you do it for that reason? What about this?"

Ultimately, I've found the biggest motivator to get my kids to do something that maybe they don't want to do in the current moment is just simply ask, "Would you do it for me? Would you just do it for me?" Being able to do that has been something that makes me realize in business sometimes all you need to do is say, "Hey, I really just need a favor. Could you do me a favor?"

## The Lesson

The biggest lesson for me in parenting is how much parenting is like running a business, in the fact that there are a couple of major elements in being a successful entrepreneur or business person. The first one is understanding leadership. Leadership isn't getting somebody else to do something. Leadership is getting somebody else to want to do something. As a parent, I have way more patience than I ever have had in my life with other people, because the beings that I'm leading are my children. They're part of me.

On the business side of things, if you're leading somebody on your team or even somebody that you're negotiating with, the question "What do you want?" is the equivalent of telling my children "Use your words."

Often in a negotiation, or in a sale, or in a leadership position, just simply saying the words, "What do you want? What is the outcome? Where are you going or where do you want to go?"

can produce massive results and insight into what you need to get done.

Not every deal will be the ideal deal or transaction that someone you are doing business with is looking for. A leader understands this and will say "I know this isn't what you expected, but would you do it this one time? Would you just do it for me? You produce amazing results."

The second thing that's been really powerful for me as a father, and also in my business life, ties right in with communication equals wealth. We communicate in two ways: internally through the 1500 words per minute that are going through our brain, and then we communicate externally to other people, which is called influence. Getting a clean slate, such as my kids, to respond to something, is a matter of understanding where are they coming from? Where's their mind at?

## Sterling's Story

My daddy makes me use the potty when I don't think I need to use the potty. Sometimes it gets me very frustrated, and I say, "Daddy, I don't have to use the potty." He says, "Well, you're dancing the potty dance right now, and it looks like you have to use the potty." I say, "I don't have to use the potty, Daddy. I don't have to use the potty." Then he'll say, "Would you please just go pretend? Would you please just go act as if you do have to go potty?" Then I'll go to the potty and I don't know why, but then when I go to the potty I have to go potty. Even though I didn't think I had to go potty, and he says just act as if you have to go potty, I find that I have to go potty. Then I go potty."

## The Lesson

Daddy has taught me a pretty good lesson in life. Even if you don't know how to do something, if you act as if you do know how to do that thing, and then you just start doing it, you will find out that you can do it. I think the biggest lesson I've learned from my daddy is act as if you can, and then you can.

## About Marshall Sylver

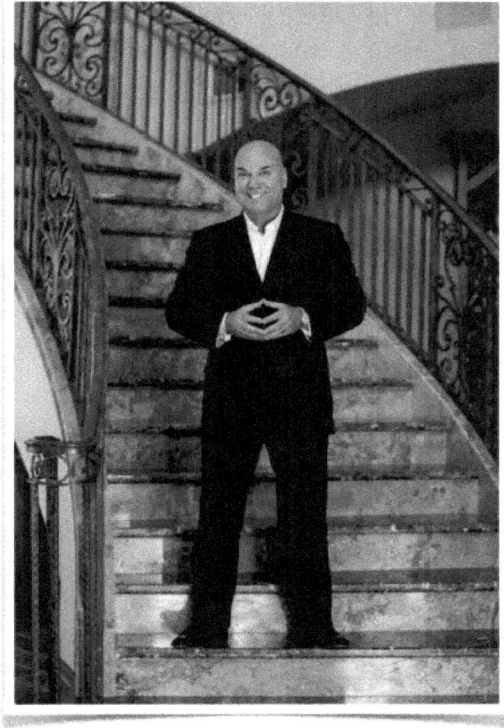

Marshall Sylver has been entertaining, educating and empowering for over 48 years.  He is the most televised hypnotist in history with multiple appearances on Late Night with David Letterman, the Late Show, Howard Stern and many more.

His books are published by Simon and Schuster and available in multiple languages worldwide. He has sold over $250,000,000 of his products and courses.

His entertainment show "Real Hypnosis Really Funny" has headlined on the mainstage of Planet Hollywood, Caesars Palace, The Palms and many more.

Whether is at his 17,000-square-foot Palace in Las Vegas, lounging at his ocean front home in Southern California or flying around on private jets to change people's lives, Marshall is a product of his product. For more information about Marshall Sylver and what he is up to go to www.Sylver.com.

## About Sterling Sylver

Sterling Marshall Sylver was born May 18, 2011. His mother, Erica, was hypnotized to give birth on his dad's birthday May 19th and missed it by just six hours. His siblings Maximus and Prosperity, like Sterling, were born via hypnosis in the master bath at their home Prosperity Palace in Las Vegas. Sterling loves being on stage, reading and being an awesome son and big brother. He is kind, smart, and very compassionate.

# Life is Like a Piece of Cheese

## Sarie's Story

My learning curve started before my daughter was even born, she was growing nicely in my tummy, and my hellish journey began!

My daughter was planned, and we were delighted and excited! I had a period of acute anxiety in my mid-twenties (that's a whole other story), and so I had started my therapeutic/personal awareness journey already. However, looking back, I was still quite emotionally naive, even four years later when I fell pregnant. I had started my training as a psychotherapist, but stopped around this time, as I had so much already to deal with. (Thankfully I went back to finish it at a later date, as it's a huge part of my business and life now!)

I had a healthy pregnancy, no issues physically, and it was all going great until I hit six months. My sister (who I am extremely close to in age and relationship), ended up being resuscitated at the hospital, and then ended up spending a while in intensive care fighting for her life – she was a very Type 1 Diabetic and we hadn't known. The stress and worry of this situation triggered all of my old anxieties, which had started to rear through pregnancy anyway (which they can tend to do); I began to feel overwhelmed. The type of overwhelm that you may recognise if you had suffered from severe anxiety, the completely irrational, out of control feelings, that can really affect your day to day functioning.

I was literally just managing to keep my head above water. I just wanted my daughter to continue to grow and arrive safely. Easy hey. Yeah right!

When my sister was still recovering, a month or so after, we got the devastating news that my dad had been diagnosed with stage four terminal cancer, and only had a matter of months to live.

My grieving process began, alongside my growing feelings of overwhelming love and protection of my unborn daughter.

A contradiction. It was both confusing and overwhelming.

## The Lesson

This is where the real lesson for me began.

Fear, joy, sadness, grief, excitement, anger and the list goes on. It was the first time properly in my life that I accepted (I didn't seem to have a choice) that I could experience these feelings all at the same time. That the highs and lows could be so extreme, yet I would survive!

I was vulnerable, yet I could still function, just about. My daughter arrived safely, and my dad was still alive. Again, the roller coaster of emotions ensued; Joy, relief, fear, and sadness.

I don't believe that becoming an entrepreneur, a business owner, whatever you want to call it, happens by accident. I think it takes certain strength of character and a whole load of determination. Being an entrepreneur can be exciting, motivating, exhilarating as well as worrying, isolating and overwhelming. It takes dedication, as it can be such a roller coaster emotionally, as well as practically. It takes a person who can find balance in their lives to avoid burnout. Someone who doesn't give up when things get difficult, and can ground themselves, when things are going great guns! Are you starting to see the parallels?

I believe that these parallels continue throughout parenthood, and that parenting definitely mirrors being in business in many ways. In fact, I see a strong relational pattern between the stages of a child's development and a growing business.

Self-awareness and knowing our vulnerabilities, which my daughter taught me in abundance, and still does, is key for a successful business. I would love to share with you now, a small insight into the stages of development we go through emotionally, so that you can also relate it to your business. (I use the stages of child development by Pam Levin as she is fab!)

**Being – This is the stage emotionally for a child from 0 to 6 months.**

Think about your business. It's the initial stage where you are so passionate and in love, and just want to be 'in your business' constantly! You don't care too much about the late nights, waking up full of ideas – it's worth it! You just do what you need to get by, but you are in 'lust' with your business, it's new and exciting, it's your baby!

**Doing – We are now talking about 6 to 18 months.**

Doing. Doing. Doing. Now you are very actively doing lots in your business. Your to-do list is growing bigger and bigger, and the newness and excitement may start becoming a chore, as you just have so much to do and explore, and not enough time! Here we also explore boundaries, work out whom we trust, while starting to get some help and support. (Hopefully!) As kids in this stage, we are separating and individuating from our parents, and it's healthy – this is where us business owners start to delegate and outsource.

**Thinking – 18 month to 3 years old.**

Here the thinking (and possibly overthinking or procrastination) really kicks in. We are thinking much more long term, and visualising our future much more clearly. We start to think more about what we really want from our future, and for our business. Our future success can rely very heavily on how we manage this stage. It might be that you change direction, or completely turn things on their head here! (You could find yourself jumping back to the being stage!)

**Identity – 3 to 6 years old.**

What kind of business and entrepreneur do you really want to be? This is where we are consolidating our story, our script, which will influence how we then survive in the business world going forward. Here we start to separate fantasy from reality, and start really making sense of things. We definitely mean business now. We really assert ourselves, and are very proud of our business and what we do.

**Skills – 6 to 12 years old.**

We become so super skilful now. This doesn't mean we weren't skilful before, but now we are really starting to consolidate and validate our earlier decisions. We are getting SO good at what we are doing now! We will continue to check in with ourselves, and our business, by keeping on testing against our existing identity, so that we can strengthen or make changes when we need to.

**And last but by no means least. Regeneration – Age 12 to 18 years.**

This is the teenage stage of your business, where you will recycle all the previous stages over and over again, building your business continuously!

Now your business may not take the same amount of years to go through these development stages as your child, and you do emotionally, but I certainly believe we transition through these stages at our own pace (I know I have and am not through them all just yet) and I have often found myself mirroring my daughter's developmental stages with my business!

You might wonder why I wanted to share these stages with you, and why this is my biggest learning from being a parent in business? I think they highlight some really important aspects to consider:

- Expect challenging and difficult times, its ok.

- Feelings are not black or white. You can be successful and vulnerable at the same time, its ok.

- One thing you can be sure of, that no matter what stage you are at and how you are finding that stage, things will CHANGE. Remember when you feel stuck or want to give up, feelings pass, and things change. Our children are a great example of this! One minute we are worrying that they are not eating enough of their vegetables, and then before we know it, we are worrying that they are not constantly in our sights! One thing is for sure, things change and often rapidly! It's ok.

- Contentment comes in all different shapes and sizes, and sometimes we need to remind ourselves of what that looks like for us, in both our personal and professional lives. Don't be led by other peoples' happiness, as it might not look the same as yours. It's ok.

- Don't do it all alone! Reach out to likeminded people. We are sociable beings, and we need connection and interaction. Go looking for it. It's ok.

## Maia's Story – What I learned from my Mum

*This has been left untouched. It was important that she did this herself for both of us, so it's literally her words.*

My mum is a therapist, so this is good because she seems to know what to do with all of my different feelings. So, when I am feeling scared to go on holiday, and leave my home, she says your home is the people you are close to, so you are safe with them. When you feel safe at home, it is because you are with the people you are comfortable with, and you know that they will protect you at home, so you should feel the same anywhere, because they will always look after you wherever you are!

My mum has told me to always speak up about what you want, or how you are feeling because if you don't, nobody can read your mind and see what you want, or how you are feeling right at that moment. Our emotions change all through the day because you could start off grumpy and feel like it could ruin your day, but one hour later, you are happy having fun with your friends, so always say what you want to say, because someone can always help!

The next thing my mum has taught me is that some of the thoughts in your head are real and some are just what we call stories and that they are not real. Sometimes I tell mum that they are real, because they feel that real in my head, but she says don't overthink things. (but sometimes they are still in my head, however they always go after a minute or two of not overthinking things, yes see it works!)

My mum has also said not to be afraid to try new things, and whenever I go to do new things I get to nervous, but today I felt brave and thought really what is the worst thing that could happen, so I went and got the end of my hair purple! (I am not sure what school will say after the holidays)

As I am getting older, I am learning a lot about life.

## The Lesson

Life is almost like a piece of cheese; it has holes in it, but it still tastes yummy!

## More from Sarie

Asking my daughter to do this, and giving her complete free reign on what she wanted to say, was an amazing experience and goes full circle. A lot of what she describes could also be a great lesson in running a business. (And maybe she will use this one-day, in her own work life!)

Now I feel I need to give a bit of a disclaimer here, as we run a business based on not being perfect parents, but being perfectly aware we are not perfect. The above makes it sound like I have done an amazing job of teaching my daughter!

Here are the bloopers– they didn't make the cut (not my choice but hers!)

What else has she learned along the way?

After two glasses of wine, adults get louder and are very annoying!

Sometimes when mummy has had a few clients, she can be quite moody!

Mum and dad both spend way too much time on their mobiles!

However, we are not going to worry too much about these things, as after all life IS like a piece of cheese!

## About Sarie and Maia Taylor

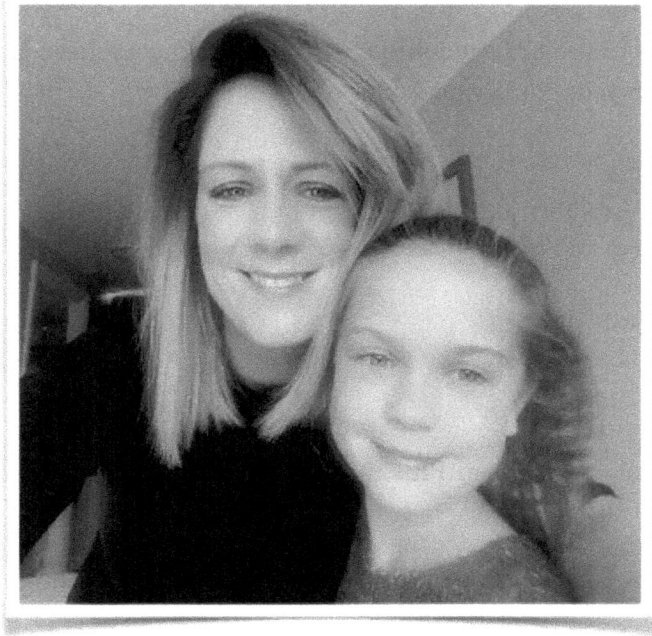

Sarie is the co-founder of Parent Plus, who offers support, coaching and therapeutic services to parents, families, and professionals in the field. Sarie also runs a private psychotherapy hypnotherapy, coaching and NLP practise, Sarie Taylor Coaching based in the UK. (Although she has clients all over the world!)

Sarie has a varied past both personally and professionally, working in prisons and probation as well as starting off in a very 'corporate' environment in recruitment. Sarie has now found her calling in life, coaching and support as well as parenting her wonderful daughter Maia.

Maia has recently turned 10 years old. Maia absolutely loves cheerleading, particularly as the flyer (basically being thrown into the air), but she also loves playing football with her local team. Maia is a very hard working, lovable and a sensitive soul who will do anything for anyone. Maia is very entrepreneurial herself and would love to set up her own website selling pajamas that children could customise for themselves. Maia has two fluffy cats, Tink and Belle!

**Website**
SarieTaylor.com
Parent-Plus.co.uk

**Our Academy**
ParentPlusAcademy.com

**Instagram**
Instagram.com/ParentPlus2015

**Twitter**
Twitter.com/SarieTaylor
Twitter.com/ParentPlus2015

**Facebook**
Facebook.com/SarieTaylorCoaching
Facebook.com/ParentPlus2015

**YouTube**
ParentPlus2015

We have so many different levels of support we can offer, from our free Facebook support group
Facebook.com/Groups/179957485693542
to our more specific support for you and your family. See what we offer and get our freebies while you are there!
ParentPlusacademy.com

# To Daddy from Gabriel

## Chad's Story – I Don't Give Up. Neither Should You.

My son Gabriel is only two years old, and you can imagine how hectic life can get. If you have kids, I'm sure you remember right when you found out you were going to have a baby you had that scared, nervous, and excited feeling inside you. Not too long after, you made that conscious decision that no matter what life could throw at you, you would always provide for your child.

For those of us that are entrepreneurs, that meant those 7-figure dreams needed to become a reality.

I began working harder and harder every day up until we had Gabriel. Looking back, that was one of the best days of my life. I love being a dad more than anything. I started taking some time off to spend with my son and watch him grow into the big boy he is today.

What I truly lost sight of?

That ambition I had before he was born. I was so caught up in being the world's best dad; I forgot that I needed to be the world's best provider too.

Business was down, we were stressed for money, but Gabriel and I were as happy as could be.

One morning Gabriel was sick, so I decided to stay home. The poor guy looked miserable, so I offered up a movie day with Dad! He shook his head no and pointed down to his blocks on the floor.

If there was one thing Gabriel loved, it was his blocks. He loves to build things. I figured why not let him play with his blocks for a little while, and eventually, he'll get bored and want to lay down.

Four hours later, I was starving, wanted food and wanted to relax. Gabriel had me building large castles and all sorts of crazy things. He kept nodding off like he wanted a nap. As I went to pick him up to put him in his crib so he could rest and get some sleep, he began to cry. This was normal for Gabriel.

Like every two-year-old, he wouldn't stop crying. Almost an hour went by, so I picked him up and put him near his blocks again. He started building away. After about 10 minutes, he nodded off and fell asleep sitting up!

Poor guy, I thought. I picked him up and put him back in his crib. I must have woken him up because as soon as his eyes opened, he looked at me, stood up and looked back at his blocks and started pointing at his blocks and stomping his feet. You know the attitude I'm talking about, don't you?

I couldn't believe this kid.

He was literally trying to build his castle and falling asleep at the same time. He'd nod off and wake himself up on accident and place a few blocks... and back to sleep he went.

I started to have a realization.

There's a lesson we can all take away from this.

My son Gabriel was built the same way I am. We both don't stop working until we're finished. We don't quit when we're tired, or when life gets hard.

This was something I had completely forgotten during the chaotic life I was living since Gabriel was born.

So, take it from Gabriel, my two-year-old boy. "I'll quit when I'm finished not when I'm tired."

I've taken this massive lesson to heart and live every day like this.

## Gabriel's Story – Monkey See, Monkey Do

Although my son is too young to really interrupt the lessons and actions I try and teach him, one thing has always been clear.

If he sees me do something, you better believe he will too.

Let me explain.

I was sitting on the couch the other night watching tv. I was kind of slouched over leaning towards the television as if whatever I was watching was pretty interesting.

I glance over and watch my son literally fall over trying to slouch like I was.

I had no choice but to laugh and ask him "Are you trying to be like Daddy?" He, of course, nodded his head and smiled.

It was adorable; it would have melted your heart too.

However, at that time I didn't really grasp the full reality of the situation that was unfolding in front of my eyes.

A few days later, a similar situation happened.

I was pacing around on the phone with a business partner discussing a deal we were working on, and I noticed that Gabriel was following me around the house. This was also normal, but that day was much different. He was holding up his toy phone, pacing around, and moving his hands around all crazy just like I do when I talk.

Out of nowhere, I hear a loud "Thud."

I looked back and saw Gabriel reaching for his toy phone. He said "Whoops," grabbed his phone, held it up to his ear, and began pacing around pretending to be talking on it.

I couldn't help but bust up laughing. He looked like a mini version of myself just pacing around the kitchen trying to close a deal.

It started to get me thinking... Do our kids really pick up everything we say and do?

## The Lesson

I more carefully consider the actions I take every single day. I want to make sure that I'm the best version of myself, or at least I'm working towards it. My son deserves the best, and I certainly won't settle for giving him anything less than that.

So, I started watching my words more carefully, my body language, how I handled my frustration and anger.

What did I learn?

That there's an entire new world when someone else is watching you. You truly do become the best version of yourself.

I started closing more deals because the words I selected were extremely precise.

I started closing more deals because my body language was on point and confident.

I started closing more deals because I started handling my frustration and anger like a true Buddha and began channeling my inner mind and canceling out the negativity.

I started closing more deals simply because I knew my son was watching.

What did I get other than more closed deals?

My son doesn't see me handle anger in a negative way.

My son doesn't watch me stress out over a deal not closing.

My son doesn't see me slouched and unconfident when I'm on the phone.

My son listens to me select words more precisely, so he too will have a good vocabulary soon enough.

You can see how becoming the very best version of yourself not only helps you in business but at home too. It helps your family grow, your communication skills, and your relationship with your children.

So, if I preach anything, it's this...

Pay attention to how you live your life, because it will make you a better version of you.

# About Chad Michael Hensley

Born November 8, 1984 in Wayne County, MI

Studied at Madonna University 2002 - 2007 B.S. Criminal Justice

CEO of NextGen Monitoring

CEO of Connectility

After college, I started my career as a Public Safety Officer at the University of Michigan serving for only a year before I took a position with the United States Government. For the next few years, I served on the Anti Terrorism - Contraband Enforcement Team with US Customs and Border Protection. Seeking a warmer climate, I resigned my position and headed south to explore the plethora of law enforcement opportunities in Texas.

During that transition, I accepted a sales position to hold me over during the hiring process with Dallas Police Dept. Quickly discovering my aptitude for sales, leadership, and team building – I decided that business was the logical career path and never looked back. Fast forward eight years and I have a beautiful fiancé and two amazing children. I have the pleasure of managing over 100 sales reps across three states and am part of a rapidly growing company that gets stronger every day! We are always looking for more talented and hungry individuals to join our team so please reach out if you'd like to be part of our movement!

### Facebook
Facebook.com/profile.php?id=1413279570

### E-Mail
Chad@ConnectedinTexas.com

### Website
ConnectedInTexas.com

## About Gabriel Alexander Hensley

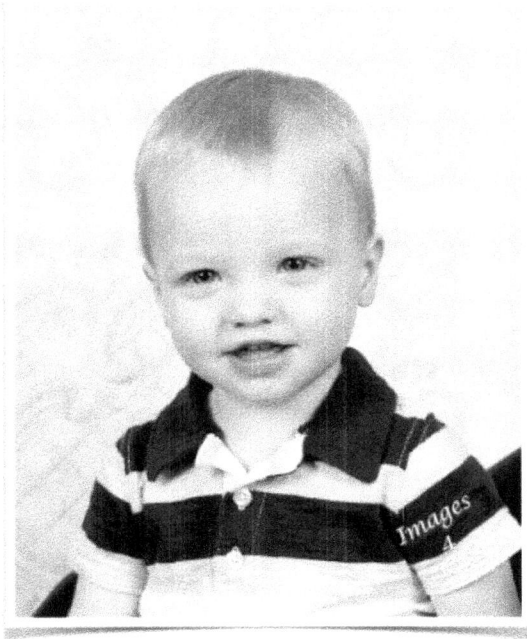

Born: November 18, 2015 in Tarrant County, TX

Studied at Primrose school 2016 - current

Gabe enjoys singing, coloring, destroying the house, pulling the cat's tail, and long walks around the neighborhood!

He has strong vocabulary skills and is a very smart little boy. His mom is a Child Psychologist, so he has quite the teacher at home. Gabe is in the 98th percentile for size among other kids his age – a big boy! Mom and Dad are already hearing the cheers at his high school football games!

# R-E-S-P-E-C-T

## Troy's Story

In 2008, during one of the worst economies of my lifetime, I lost everything. At the time, I had multiple cabinet shops, construction companies, and land development companies. In a matter of 30 days, I went from 'about to retire early' to losing everything, as millions of dollars' worth of deals that we had in escrow, about to close, fell apart, one by one.

I was left holding the bag on millions of dollars of debt, which cost me everything. The stress of it all took more than just my financial being and material things, my marriage of seven years came to a screeching halt as well. Fortunately, through it all, I've maintained an incredible relationship with my children, though complicated by the fact that they live in Brazil with their mom, my ex.

Rebuilding an entire livelihood from nothing is not trivial, especially when you're also making the transition into a new line of work, shifting into online digital entrepreneurialism for the first time, doing it overseas, and starting out hundreds of thousands of dollars in debt while going through a divorce and struggling just to keep your kids in private school. Trust me, in Brazil, public school was not an option.

I've created five different companies since that time and while the journey through entrepreneurialism has not been easy, I wouldn't trade it for anything. Along the way, I learned to invest in me first and foremost. I began attending training events, hired personal business, marketing, and life coaches and have invested in various masterminds — all for the improvement of myself and my businesses.

As my oldest son, Thales, got more and more interested in what I do, I've involved him more in my businesses and work. After he graduated high school, he came to live with me in Florida. His desire was that good ole dad was going to pay his way through college. Let's just say we had different goals.

I intended to teach him to fish, not give him the fish. So, I told him the harsh news — that I wouldn't pay for his college, but that he could work for me as an unpaid intern and learn how to make his own money if he wanted. It was not the answer he was looking for.

He pouted and moped around for a couple of weeks, testing me to see if I'd change my mind. Then he realized he really didn't have much of choice in the matter and began to intern for me.

He saw firsthand just how hard I worked and it was a challenge to get him to shift his mindset about work and what it meant to be an entrepreneur. So, I took him to one of my masterminds that I attend down in Boca Raton. For years, I've been making the four-hour drive down, and another four hours back, each month, investing in myself, investing in this mastermind.

When I asked around the table if the rest of the members minded if my son sit in the back and just be a "fly on the wall" and observe, they rejected the idea. Instead, they insisted he sit at the table with the rest of us and participate as an individual member of the mastermind.

My son was just amazed at all that he was learning, and a little bit overwhelmed that these very successful 7- and 8-figure marketers would be devoting time to him. Several of the people, as we went around the table, forfeited their time and yielded it to him instead.

When the event was over, we jumped in the car and started to drive home. My son began to talk all about what he had learned, and I quickly shut him down. Instead of talking, I told him, "Pull out your journal and just write. Write it all out. Get everything out of your head, everything you've learned, everything you're feeling, just get it down on paper. Then we'll talk."

He spent the next hour or so just writing in his journal. Then when he was complete, I gave him one final task. I asked him, "if you had to sum up this experience in just one word, what would that word be?"

He thought about it for a long time, then said, "Respect."

## The Lesson

I was a bit perplexed by his response, so I asked him to explain. He then went into a long conversation and very eloquently explained to me how his biggest impression was that these people, people he didn't know, people that charged $100's of dollars an hour for their time, people that had made millions of dollars, had treated him as an equal.

He was almost brought to tears as he described how good it made him feel that they, despite having the right to in his mind, didn't talk down to him, but looked to help him, to serve him and to even learn from him. He was just flabbergasted at the whole experience.

I learned a lot that day from my son. I learned the humility of his insights and to never forget where I had come from, who I was serving, and to meet them at their level. Over the next four hours on the long drive home, he continued to open my mind by his takeaways.

I found myself not just hearing him, but listening to him and the very deep insights that he had made through this experience. That day was the first day that I began to see him as more of a friend than my son. It was also the beginning of a journey that the two of us have undertaken, not only working together but also learning from each other.

Today, my son is my number one go-to guy in my company, my right-hand man. At 19, he's got the marketing mind, business sense and maturity that I'd put up against most 30-year olds, and it all began, that day, when his eyes were opened to what is possible, and my heart was opened to what he was capable of.

At just 19, he is an integral part of my businesses, holding key positions in two of them and even managing a small team. He's no longer an "unpaid" intern, but a well-paid member of my team. He's now saving to purchase his first investment property, which he'll probably do before he's 20. I continue to learn from him each day we work together, as he does from me.

A father couldn't be more proud.

## Thales's Story – The Ten Thousand Feet County Fair Wall

It was that time of the year again, summer!

The air was hot in Northern California, the sky was blue and I could run around with my dogs in the grass all day long. At night, I would play with my Legos and video games way past my bedtime and eventually, when the time was right, the County fair would show up in town and brighten my vacation days.

The cotton candy, the rides, hot dogs, clowns... all of that was just so awesome as a six-year-old (and it still is as a nineteen-year-old)! I remember I even used to compete with my friends on who could ride the most rides. Those were the days...

But this year I was about to face the most difficult thing in my entire life (I was six, life wasn't that hard), I was going to go beyond my comfort zone! Yes, you read that right, the six-year-old was about to do something he had never done before, shocker!

Now don't think I just decided that year I was about to do something extraordinarily different that I had never done before... this was the work of something beyond my control, this was the work of:

A Dad.

Didn't you just LOVE when your Dad pushed you to do stuff you didn't want to?

I sure didn't!

But I am glad that he did push me that day at the fair...

I used to watch the other kids climb up this huge climbing rock. They would climb up to the top and hit a big red buzzer that rang loudly to show everybody they made it to the top.

I wanted to give it a try and hit the buzzer, so my Dad (Troy Broussard) paid for me to go once. The first eight steps were easy, the wall didn't even seem that big when I was down below, but when I was in the middle of it and looked down, I tightened up and froze.

The wall seemed like it grew ten thousand feet and was somehow bigger than when I was on the ground, this wasn't as easy as it seemed… I grew more and more afraid the longer I stood up there and eventually I just dropped, and the safety rope took me back to solid ground.

When the rock climbing guy unhooked me from the safety harness, I ran to my Mom, and I was done with that thing!

But my Dad had other plans…

I don't recall his exact words, but I do remember him saying something like this:

"Thales, you're going to climb that wall today, and you're gonna hit that button no matter how many times I have to pay for you to climb that thing!"

Obviously, I tried to get my Mom to save me from that situation - since I couldn't sweet talk myself out of that one, maybe she could. But not even Mom could help me out, my Dad had made up his mind.

She fought and fought with my Dad, but he was determined to get me up that wall! He reached in his wallet and pulled out a

$100 bill and told me he could pay for me to climb that wall all day long if that's what it took.

After a while, I stopped crying and gave it another try... but this time the rock wall already seemed ten thousand feet tall from the ground up, I knew what was waiting for me up there (fear).

I climbed up less than half and gave up. My Dad paid for another try.

I climbed up almost half this time. My Dad paid for another try.

I climbed up half and let go. My Dad paid for another try.

Oh my god, he really wasn't going to give up on me till I pushed that buzzer at the top!

I hated him at that point. I was mad, and humiliated that I was the only kid who couldn't climb that thing. He just kept sending me back up there to fail... but he knew that I could do it, he just needed me to believe in myself like he believed in me.

Then on the fourth try or so he pulled me to the side and said:

"Thales, I know you're afraid but you've got to push past that! Stop looking down, I know that's what's scaring you the most... when you start getting scared just focus on the buzzer, keep climbing and DON'T LOOK DOWN!"

On the very next try after he talked to me, I started climbing the wall with an eye full of determination (and tears). This time I knew I could do it... inch by inch, step by step I crept past the halfway point... I knew I was higher than I had ever been before.

I started shaking, tightening up and almost froze but I didn't stop. I knew that if I stopped, I wouldn't move again. All I could see as I continued to climb was the big red buzzer staring me right in the face.

Little by little, I got closer, and closer, and closer - until I reached and smashed the buzzer and heard that beloved buzzing noise I so desperately wanted to hear!

I remember holding down that button for a solid ten seconds, overlooking the whole fair, seeing my Mom and Dad cheering me on and looking at the kids below me.

I owned that buzzer. I owned that wall!

I felt like the king of the world, I was the king of the world that day - and I'm pretty sure my Dad felt the same.

## The Lesson

What I learned that day was priceless and timeless. I can replay this memory for as long as I live and feel that same sensation of when I was at the top of the wall.

That day, my Dad taught me that as long as you believe in yourself, no matter how many times you fail, if you want something bad enough, if you believe in yourself like I did, you can do and have anything you want - it's just a matter of time when you'll get it.

You just have to block out the world sometimes, the negative comments, even your own negative thoughts, and focus on what counts. And getting out of your comfort zone every once in a while won't kill you and might even make you feel more alive!

So, the next time you're faced with a ten-thousand-foot wall, just know it's much smaller than you think and you'll get to the top... just use failure as a "stepping stone" to success!

# About Troy A. Broussard

Troy Broussard is an experienced Marketer, Entrepreneur, and Best Selling Author. He has created five businesses in the past five years in the Services, Coaching and SaaS spaces. He has extensive backgrounds in product creation, high ticket sales and service businesses, systems, databases, and programming.

Troy's passion is in creating efficient business systems and automation solutions that allow small business owners to spend much more of their time working on their business instead of in their business. He is the father of four and travels extensively between his homes on the East Coast, West Coast, and Brazil.

To reach Troy, you can contact him at troy@ismastery.com.

## About Thales G. Broussard

Thales G. Broussard (Pronounced TAh-LIS)

Born in Brazil on October 29th, 1997. Thales moved to the USA when he was five years old and back to Brazil when he was 11. But ever since he experienced America and the American dream, he's had a burning passion for the American Internet entrepreneur lifestyle (mostly inspired by his Dad, Troy Broussard).

Thales enjoys figuring out how stuff works (reverse engineering is a must for this skill), loves learning new things (currently self-taught programmer in the making) and is amazed at what the Internet is capable of in the right hands.

# Quality Uncomplicated

If we really watch and listen to our kids, they can teach us many things. What I didn't expect is that I'd become an entrepreneur because of my son.

## Nancy's Story

For the first seven years of Griffin's life, I was a single mom. That had its challenges and rewards. When he was two and a half years old, I needed to go back to work. Found a great job – easy. Finding childcare – not easy. Actually, awful. I thought I was doing the right thing. I looked at reputable daycares – they were full of seemingly happy kids and appeared good from the outside. It's when I went inside and met with the staff that things started to go wrong. There were all sorts of "forced" items that I wasn't okay with – forced nap time, Griffin wasn't a great sleeper. Forced food menu, i.e., milk with every meal, we don't drink milk. When I raised concerns about these easy-to-accommodate things, I was told: "That's the way that it is." I can appreciate the need to provide a schedule that suits the center as a whole, but I couldn't fathom what that day would look like for my son. I ran through the scenario over and over in my head picturing him crying during nap time and being forced to lay down. Would they understand him? Would they comfort him?

Would he just be left inconsolable wondering where his mother is? These thoughts made me sick to my stomach.

I then found a woman who looked after a few kids in her home. Sabrina was kind and understanding. She would mother Griffin the same as I would, with the same consideration. I could finally take a deep breath and confidently go to work without feeling guilty. And I could send my own mother home, who was on an extended stay with me while I searched for childcare – this process took me five months.

There were lots of ups and downs with Griffin's development and the support he received around that – but as for his care while I was at work – that was perfect. He was at his home away from home and thriving. I was working, independent and happy. This was all good until he entered public school in first grade. I honestly thought life was going to get easier; childcare was going to get easier. After all, Griffin was in school from 9 a.m. to 3 p.m. The need for childcare was minimal. Boy, was I wrong.

Enter the world of after-school programs, or as they're more commonly called now out-of-school programs. If I thought the quality of childcare was a problem when Griffin was younger, I had no idea how much worse it could get as he got older. Now I had to find a school that had an out-of-school program in or near it. The school two blocks from our home was the obvious choice. I called the program that happened to run out of the gym after school. I wanted to understand what Griffin would be doing after school and really wanted to get a feel for the place so I set up an appointment to meet the owner. I waited and waited; nobody showed up. In the distance, I could see a group of kids running wild, and as they got closer, I noticed a young girl, possibly 20 years old with them. I assumed she was in charge. I told her that I was there to meet the owner. She shrugged saying that she didn't know anything about it. She didn't offer me a tour, didn't offer me any information, didn't offer to pass the message along that I had come by. I started to feel sick. Here we go again...

I found another school that was close *'ish*, but still feasible for me to drive Griffin every day and still get to work on time. They had a program that was run by a reputable company. This company had huge recreation centers all over the city. They had everything from state of the art gyms and pools, and provided lessons in everything from soccer to basket weaving. I had no idea they offered their programs through satellite locations in local schools. This was it! I was completely relieved and began breathing again. Or so I thought...

One month into the school year, I received a note from the program's head office stating that the following year the program would be decreasing their services due to lack of necessity. What?!? There were 30 kids in the program, what lack of necessity? It went on to say that they would no longer offer a place for kids before school and the after-school portion would be shortened. No, no, no. This was not going to be okay. I worked for big corporation, there was no way I could drop my son off to school at 9 a.m. and then drive across town. I would be strolling into the office at 10 a.m.

My job started at 8:30 a.m. and our sales meetings were mandatory. Not meeting my job requirements would surely get me fired. I was a single mom; losing my job was not an option.

I asked the Principal for a meeting and voiced my concerns over this. Truly I was panicked, and I was hoping that he would have a solution. At one point during the meeting, he looked and me and said, "Why don't you do it?" I know he wasn't being sarcastic or flippant. I had some valid concerns and some great ideas. Clearly, he added the two and decided that I would be a good solution. There was one tiny problem: I didn't want to do it. I wanted someone else to do it, and do it right.

I believe that entrepreneurs are born, not made, and it was sometime after this meeting that the entrepreneur in me emerged. I was restless over this issue. Every day I picked up my son from this program, I noticed yet another thing I would change *if I were running the program*. The 19-year old program leader that supervised the children by having her head down looking at her cell phone. The playground supervisor that didn't notice that I picked up Griffin from the playground and assumed when he was missing that he was okay. The broken toys and a pile of coloring sheets as the only option for play. The blue Kool-Aid that was served as the beverage of the "nutritious snack" really pushed me over the edge. This was what my son was doing every day? This was not good enough. This was not the environment that I wanted for my son. Maybe I *could* do this? I'm getting pissed off about it, so maybe I can be the one to fix it.

That night, I printed the government regulations for an out-of-school program. It was 54 pages of sections and sub-sections of regulations including things like not smoking in the program to square footage of acceptable window surfaces. I couldn't make a program out of this. This stuff was obvious. No smoking, check. Now what? This was not for me. I couldn't make heads or tails from this, and I certainly didn't find any guidance or inspiration of what to do next.

Griffin and I would frequent bookstores and coffee shops on the weekends. We would read, chat and spend quality time together. It was during this regular occurrence that the inspiration for Summit Kids happened. We were in Starbucks, me with a venti coffee and Griffin with a cookie. The place was almost empty; we had the pick of seating. As I was putting sugar in my coffee, I noticed something that I had seen a dozen times before. Griffin walked through the coffee shop past all the tables and chairs to the only leather, over-sized, club chair. He was pleased with himself as he sat on this huge chair. He was comfortable, and this made him happy.

That was it! I was looking at this the wrong way all this time. I knew what I needed to do.

That night after Griffin went to bed, I took out a pad of paper and started to write. I poured all my hopes and dreams for Griffin onto that paper. I listed all the things I wanted him to experience. I wrote about the ideal environment and different settings, the people that I wanted him to be around, the influences, the opportunities, and the things he needed to learn. I wrote and wrote. I then took out the 54 pages of government regulations and married the two. All of the do's and don'ts from the government paired with the hopes and dreams of a mother. For the first time, I had hope that I could create the world that I wanted for Griffin. I didn't need feel guilty or be held hostage by what was lacking. I could change all of that.

To be honest, I didn't even know what an entrepreneur was. Sure, I knew what the definition of the word was, but in my mind, it was someone else; it was people that you read about, Richard Branson or Steve Jobs. I was just a mom. I was tired of being unsatisfied, and tired of being pissed off. I had no idea that the entrepreneur in me was surfacing. I needed to fix a problem. I needed a great place for my son, and I knew I wasn't the only parent that wanted great things for my child – I knew there had to be more of us.

## The Lesson

Griffin had no idea that day he opened my eyes to the very simple realization that children are people too. They have the same need for comfort, the same need for acceptance, and they have the same reaction to something beautiful or soft or kind. I realized that day that the issue that I had with all of the child-centric environments of which I had come across was that they were all institutional in their approach. Functional, rigid and maintained the minimal standards for operating. Not one place, except for Sabrina's home, was comfortable or considered the needs of the individual child.

Summit Kids was launched six months later in September 2009. As soon as I knew the solution to the problem that plagued me for all those years, I was on a fast-track to get it done. We opened our doors with 37 kids and I hired three program leaders to work there. Today, we have 14 locations, we serve 700+ kids daily, and we have sister programs that offer great programming to children 12 months to 17 years old. It seems there were other parents out there that wanted someone to offer them a place that would be more like home – comfortable. And offer great opportunities, care, and consideration.

Griffin continues to be the guiding force of my company. Every scenario is met with the question: If you had children, would you want this for them? Indifference is unacceptable. Mediocrity is unacceptable. We're raising humans to be great humans, and the only way to do this is with love.

## Griffin's Story – Finding My Tribe and Being Polite

I travel with my parents a lot. Sometimes for vacation, other times for business conferences, and often a combination of the two.

My parents treat conference trips as an extension of school or work. I'm not old enough to attend many of the actual conferences, so while my parents are in the sessions, I use that time to study for exams or work on any school projects that I have. I meet them during coffee breaks and lunch breaks. I hang out with the other conference participants and get to meet really cool people. I've met people from all over the world – entrepreneurs, business leaders, authors, speakers, and inventors. I've met some world-famous people like Robin Sharma and Steve Wozniak. At first, I thought my parents brought me with them to these conferences because they didn't have anyone else to watch me while they weren't home. My mom told me that wasn't at all the reason. She said that there is proof that you turn into the five people you spend the most time with – proximity of influence, I think she called it. She also said that it was important that I meet and hang out with great people. I was surprised to learn that many of these people were just like me. They struggled in school, some had learning disabilities, some were misdiagnosed, misunderstood. Some struggle socially or struggle to simply find that place that they belonged. What is really cool is that they found something or some way to not only make it work, but to make it big. I think my mom was trying to show me that there's possibility, even if there are things that you struggle with.

My parents started to bring me to these conferences when I was in junior high. I guess they must have known how badly I was struggling. The teachers didn't understand me, and I didn't understand all the rules that seemed to change according to the day or the class or the teacher. I also realized quickly that "extra" help was just something that friends would tease me about. Like I wasn't feeling bad enough that I couldn't get what my teachers were talking about, but now I'm the kid with "accommodations." No thanks. I learned how to get through on my own. I was failing miserably, but I was surviving and I knew that if I didn't complain nobody would notice. I guess my parents did notice, but instead of making a big deal about the school and my friends, my mom just went to work finding better environments for me – places where I would thrive.

The first change I made was that I joined the Royal Canadian Army Cadet Corps when I was 12. Finally, a place that I could feel successful. Instantly I loved everything about it. The uniform, the procedure and most of all the other kids. Everyone here excels at their own pace. It's no big deal if you're not promoted as fast as someone else, no big deal if you need extra help on something. Judgement free, finally.

The second change was getting accepted at a private school for learning disabilities. To look at us, you can't tell we have learning disabilities. Some are dyslexic, and others like me have attention issues. Funny thing is if I like the school topic I don't have any problems paying attention. If I don't like it or if we're going too slow and I'm bored, I don't pay attention at all. Again, no judgment here. I'm no longer the bad kid because I can't concentrate. They accept this and work with me; they don't try to get me to change.

The third change was attending the conferences. Seeing how these really cool people also struggled when they were my age and now are super successful. And super rich! – now that's cool!

# The Lesson

I didn't realize it at the time, but my mom was setting me up to be surrounded by positive people. People who were just like me and didn't judge me – my tribe. She was creating the environment that she knew I needed to thrive.

Something about me that you'll notice if you meet me is that I always say please and thank you – no matter what. My mom taught me that, but I don't really remember when exactly, I think I was really little. I didn't think that being polite and respectful was a big deal, don't get me wrong, I know it's important but what I didn't realize is that being polite is so uncommon for young people, teenagers – kids my age. I guess people don't associate that when you don't have manners, it is the same as being disrespectful. Let me explain. Every single time – I'm not exaggerating – that we go to a restaurant, hotel, or travel on a plane, the adults that I interact with are always shocked that 1) I can speak for myself (more on this later) and 2) I am polite. I get comments like, "Wow, you're so polite!" Recently when flying across the country alone, the flight attendant stopped me on the way off the plane to tell me that it was a surprise to her and a pleasure to serve "such a polite young man." To which I responded, "Thank you!"

I've now started to watch how people talk to each other, young and old. It's true, people aren't polite or have good manners all the time. How can you say please and thank you to the barista at Starbucks when you're either talking on your cell phone or looking down while texting? I'm almost 15 years old, and I love my phone, but I think that's rude.

I mentioned earlier that I can speak for myself. My mom taught me that. She created a successful business by giving kids environments where they can speak for themselves and say what they like and what they don't like. She gives them the ability to be heard. Even if it's just silly kid-talk, she makes sure that someone is there, present, listening. She makes sure that kids have all the comfort, opportunities, and consideration that adults automatically get. I'm not talking about getting "participation awards" or coddling – she just treats them like humans, with the same needs and wants as everyone else. I think those are the basics.

It's funny when we go somewhere like a restaurant, barber, doctor, or anywhere really where the adults start talking to her like I'm not in the room. She'll stop them, point to me and tell them to speak to me directly. I like this. It gives me the confidence to handle any situation just by speaking up. It makes me feel like I'm just as important as adults are and that my opinion is important too.

I don't always say Please and Thank You just because it's polite. I really do feel grateful for any person who spends the time and cares to do something for me. I know that not everyone has the opportunities or privilege that I have. I've travelled with my parents, and I know that I'm lucky to live the life that I have in Canada. We have this tradition, more like a habit of asking each other "best part." When we go for dinner, to a movie, travel, see something, do something, or experience something, we ask each other, "What was your best part?" I like doing that. We each take turns sharing what our favorite part of something – to me that's gratitude.

I hear my mom at work all the time telling people that she loves them or appreciates them – her staff, her clients and other people she does business with. It feels good when I hear her do this, even if it's not to me, so it must feel good to the other people too. I'm proud of her for being like that.

So back to the beginning of my story – please and thank you. I don't think this should be so uncommon. Maybe if people just started with those little words, they would end up feeling grateful. And if they felt grateful, they would have more respect for others. Maybe a simple please and thank you can make the world a better place. I'd like that please.

Thank you ~ Griffin.

# About Nancy E. Klensch

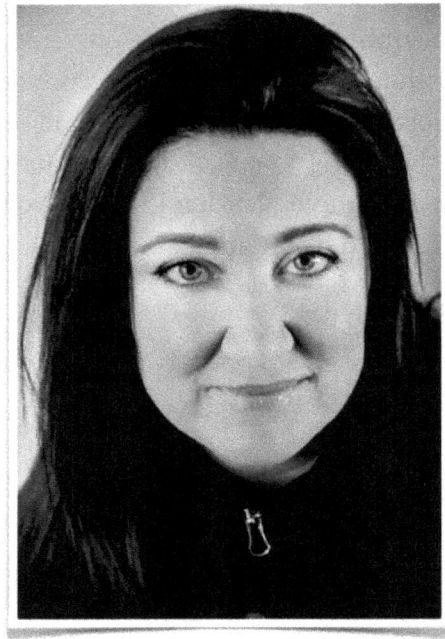

Nancy is a successful entrepreneur who is the innovator, creator, co-owner and President of Summit Kids. As a motivated presence in the industry, Nancy has very quickly changed the face of supplemental learning by creating campus environments that meet the social, emotional, physical, and developmental needs of school-aged children. She takes a holistic approach to all of her interactions—from a community stakeholder liaison to inspirational mentor and leader.

Her corporate vision is limitless with an aggressive development plan to expand globally. Nancy is philanthropic by nature, and when she's not working front-line with program participants, building her community relationships or promoting Summit Kids' corporate development, you can find her fundraising or educating the public about many causes close to her heart.

Since creating Summit Kids, Nancy has been nominated twice for Calgary's Top 40 Under 40, recognized as Business in Calgary's 2016 Business Leader, was the recipient of the Alberta Women Entrepreneurs 2017 Upsurge Award and Nominee for the EY Entrepreneurial Winning Woman Program. Summit Kids is ranked #116 on the PROFIT 500 list as one of Canada's Fastest-Growing Companies.

Nancy lives in Calgary, Alberta Canada with her husband and business partner Tyler Alton and her son Griffin.

**Twitter**
Twitter.com/Summit_Kids

**Facebook**
Facebook.com/SummitKidsyyc

**Websites**
SummitKids.ca
NekGroup.ca
NancyKlensch.com

## About Griffin Heckford

Griffin is a 14-year-old, tenth grade student at Rundle Academy in Calgary, Alberta, Canada. Griffin's love of the military started when he joined the 1292 Royal Canadian Army Cadet Corps, Lord Strathcona's Horse when he was 12. He quickly found success in both the drill & ceremony team and the marksmanship team. When Griffin isn't at the military base practicing, he enjoys snow-boarding and playing video games. He is a dog lover, world traveler, avid reader and moviegoer. Griffin is the founding inspiration for the award-winning out-of-school program Summit Kids based out of Calgary, Alberta, Canada.

# Be Relentless in Pursuits

## Jason and Nandi's Story

When we walked into the kitchen, we saw empty wrappers on the floor next to a make-shift tower that had been constructed next to the fridge from the floor all the way up to the top cabinet.

The bottom level was a chair on top of which was a stool and then a box that looked suspiciously like the one we keep next to our bedside, all the way across the house, where we store the books we read before bed, the essential oils that help us sleep, the charging cords for our phones, and other such stuff.

Curious, we went to our room to check the scene and found what had been the contents of the box now dumped out in a trail leading from the bedside to the bedroom door.

He had asked us for another "wozenge" just a few moments earlier and, in a show of solidarity, we both answered "No," because we don't like him eating a lot of sugar, even when it's in the all-natural, essential oil based lozenges we get through dōTERRA.

But our three-year-old LOVES them, especially the spicy ones, and he is RELENTLESS about having one whenever he wants.

So, despite our denial, he devised a plan, gathered materials, and executed it perfectly.

The little shit, needing one more level to reach the high cabinet where the lozenges were located, had remembered the box in our bedroom and retrieved it when we weren't looking.

Having made his tower, he climbed it to the top, got what he was after, and made out like a damn bandit.

We found him hiding in the corner of his room with a mouth full of lozenges, drool all over his face, and a big ass grin from ear to ear, knowing full well he had outsmarted us and concerned very little about the consequences.

He knew what he wanted and was neither willing to take "no" for an answer, wait for anyone to get it for him, nor let ANY obstacle stand in his way; not distance, height, gravity, or the prospect of punishment.

That's what we adults call "REAL Commitment" – which is simply deciding what you want, declaring what you will do (at least to yourself, if not to others), and then following through with resourceful action UNTIL you get it, damn the obstacles that are in the way.

## The Lesson

Probably more than anything else, our children have taught us to BE RELENTLESS IN PURSUITS, both personal and professional – to proceed with our eye on what we want, to never take "no" for an answer, to take MASSIVE action, to get back up when we get knocked down, and to ALWAYS be intelligently resourceful and flexible in our approach, UNTIL we have it.

Tony Robbins calls it "The Ultimate Success Formula" and it's just one example of the kind of stuff that kids are born with, innately, that we adults too often condition out of them (because it can be inconvenient and even exhausting), not realizing how critical it will be in their ability to succeed and lead in adulthood.

No one needs to convince a little child to go after what they want because they're simply wired to GO FOR IT come hell or high water.

Human beings are born to BE RELENTLESS in pursuit of their needs, desires, and goals!

A man or woman with a deep desire and a REAL Commitment will take control of and manipulate the elements, the environment, other living things, especially our own kind, and whatever we must, whenever we must, to get our needs met, to get what we want, to get our way, to succeed in our mission, and to fulfill our purpose – to live, learn, love, hunt, gather, create, connect, reproduce, feel, grow, contribute, and more.

My wife and I experience our sons seeing and declaring what they want, going for it boldly, never giving up, and we are inspired to do the same as a man and woman, as a husband and wife, as parents, and as entrepreneurs committed to creating value and leaving this world somehow better than we found it.

## Bodhi's Story – Dinosaur See, Dinosaur Do

I'm super passionate about dinosaurs and prehistoric creatures.

My mom and dad taught me how to read and a love for learning before my first birthday and, ever since they got me my first dinosaur encyclopedia when I was three years old, I've known that I'm going to be a paleontologist when I grow up!

Even now, it's normal to find me either sitting somewhere reading from one of my many books and encyclopedias on the subject, listening to an audiobook or podcast about dinos, or rereading Jurassic Park for the 500th time (if I'm not busy digging a hole in the backyard with a rock hammer) – LOL!

You might even overhear me sharing something I've learned with anyone who'll listen; like, did you know that the massive titanosaur, Argentinosaurus huinculensis (don't worry, my mom and dad can't pronounce it either), was the largest dinosaur ever discovered and is estimated to have been 96.4 metric tons and 39.7 meters long?

Pretty cool, huh?

Yep, dinosaurs and prehistoric creatures are the center of my universe!

Fortunately, my parents are dreamers and pursuers of dreams themselves, so they encourage me to go after whatever I want in life and they support me in any and every way they can.

But, being entrepreneurs who believe there's little (if any) wisdom in the old advice that young people should "go to school, get a degree, and get a good job," my mom and dad see many challenges with my choice of profession and are doing their best to prepare me for what lies ahead.

The reality is that there are only about 100 paleontologists working in the world today and only 40 of those are digging for dinosaurs each year; most paleontological work gets done by volunteers.

Just to become one, I'll need a doctoral degree or at least a master's, which means I'll have to pay a load of money to go to college and work VERY hard for a minimum of six to eight years studying, not only the usual stuff, but also LOTS of mathematics, like statistics, science, biology, and as much as I can about living animals.

After that, I'll have to write a looooooong paper, do LOTS of dirty work for my professors, and pay loads MORE money to complete my degree.

Only then will I be a paleontologist and lucky if I can find a job.

Just like in many other degree-dependent professions, in the field of paleontology, there are many more degreed professionals than there are jobs to be had.

Of course, my mom and dad say that if it's what I love, what I want, and if I'm willing to pay the price and do the work, then I absolutely should go for it with their full support, but on my own terms with as much control and influence over HOW I do it as possible.

Just the same as it was important to them that I learn to read early and develop a love for learning itself, it's always been important to my mom and dad that I learn business and how I can use it as a vehicle for leveraging my passions to create value, print my own money, and create a powerful, unconstrained, and unlimited life that I love.

Fortunately for them and their concerns, I also took on (almost) as much interest in business as I did in dinosaurs at a very early age.

When I was about four and a half years old, I went to my dad and said, "Dad, I want my own business like you and mom have!"

As a homeschooled kid who's never spent a minute in daycare, I had been watching my parents start businesses, create valuable content based on their knowledge, experience, and expertise, create systems and structures for delivering value to their clients and customers, create marketing campaigns, conduct sales calls, and more, daily.

I saw their example and, like most young kids, I wanted to be like my mom and dad.

Excited by my question, my dad replied, "That's great Bodhi! What kind of value would you like to offer and to who?"

Of course, I answered, "I want to teach kids about dinosaurs and prehistoric creatures!"

So, my dad and I gathered my books and encyclopedias around a white board and made an outline of five key lessons, including 1) What Are Dinosaurs, 2) The Dino's World, 3) Dinos vs. Prehistoric Creatures, 4) The Dino's Diet, and 5) How Dinos Died, plus some bonus content.

From start to finish, my dad made sure I participated in every aspect of creating and launching the business; from creating the content to setting up a hosting account to choosing a domain name to installing WordPress to building the website to scripting, recording (I got to read from a teleprompter – so cool!), editing, and uploading the videos, and launching, marketing, and selling the final product

DinosaursAreDinomite.com (shameless plug).

At that moment, at four and half years old, with the help of my dad, I had started a business around my passion, around what I LOVE, and I was officially a value producing, income earning, entrepreneur, which transformed what was possible for me and for my career as a paleontologist forever!

Now, at nine years old, my goal isn't merely to become a paleontologist, but to make $1,000,000 or more by my 20th birthday, pay for my paleontology degree myself, own my own quarry (that's a fancy name for a dig site), hire and support my own team of experts and volunteers, build my own museum, and live my life making new discoveries, filling my museum with fossils, doing research that contributes new understanding and corrects misinformation, and HOPEFULLY, someday, build my own REAL LIFE Jurassic Park.

RAAWWWOOAAAR!!!

## The Lesson

Something I've learned from my mom and dad being entrepreneurs is, if you want to be wealthy in every way possible and totally free as a result, all you need to do is find ways to add value to others and BE RELENTLESS IN THAT PURSUIT.

Most people don't realize you can learn how to transform your interests, knowledge, experiences, hobbies, expertise, and passions into products and services that people want or need; and that making money can be as easy as investing time and energy into experiencing and learning more about what you love and then passing that on as valuable expertise to others.

If you want to have maximum control and influence over your life, your career or profession, your freedom to learn, grow, and contribute, and your future, then you must have maximum control and influence over your income; and the best way to have that is by building businesses.

Make your work your play and your play your work.

# About Jason and Nandi Moore

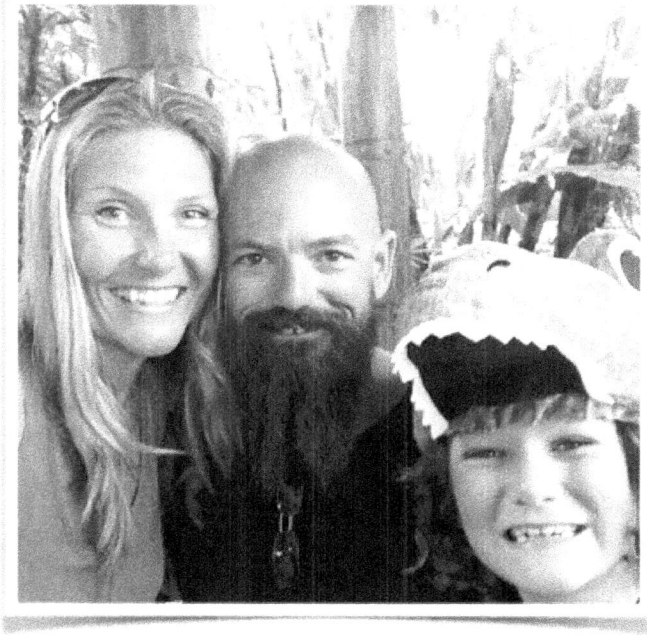

Husband and Wife, Dad and Mom, Athletes, Transformational Coaches, Breakthrough Facilitators and Adventure Guides on the greatest journey of all — life and relationships.

From their home in The Florida Keys, Jason and Nandi help struggling men and women transform the secret hell of their mediocre life and miserable marriage into a truly magnificent life and love affair.

After 12 years of living in a secret hell and pretending all was well, their relationship ended when Nandi walked out with their youngest son in tow. Life, as they knew it, appeared to be over.

It was a deep pit, but instead of giving up, they were willing to stop and ask three powerful questions: "WHO AM I BEING that it is this way?", "WHAT DO I REALLY WANT, if not this?", and "WHAT AM I COMMITTED TO doing about it?" They got clear, made a decision and a real commitment, took relentless action in pursuit of forgiveness, and everything transformed.

Exactly nine months later, they had "re-birthed" their relationship into something new, independent and free of the past. A seemingly impossible dream come true, they now enjoy an extraordinary marriage — a truly magnificent, relentless, and unconditional love affair and partnership in a shared mission to help others create similar breakthroughs in their *Awaken Hero™/Awaken Lover™* programs.

Need help? Connect with Jason and Nandi and JOIN THEIR TRIBE of Awakening HEROES and LOVERS:

*For Men:*

**Facebook**
Facebook.com/AwakenTheHero

**Personal Coaching**
AwakenHeroAcademy.com

**Entry Level Mastermind**
AwakenHeroAlliance.com

**Free Group**
AwakenHeroGroup.com

*For Women:*

**Facebook Page**
Facebook.com/AwakenTheLover

**Personal Coaching**
AwakenLoverAcademy.com

**Entry Level Mastermind**
AwakenLoverAlliance.com

**Free Group**
AwakenLoverGroup.com

## About Bodhi Shonin Moore

Bodhi Shonin Moore, the name says it all. "Bodhi" means "awakened or enlightened" and "Shonin" means "teacher." Bodhi is a super cool kid, adventurer, educator and entrepreneur living in The Florida Keys who is passionate about dinosaurs, prehistoric creatures, animals and nature and who loves living, learning and sharing his life, knowledge, and experiences with others, especially other kids, through his businesses.

Want to Learn More about *Dinosaurs Are DINOmite*™, *DINOmite Apparel*™, *Club DINOmite*™ and Bodhi's other adventures? Connect with him on his Facebook page at Facebook.com/BodhiShonin and on the web at BodhiShonin.com

# Work/Life Balance is a Lie

## Matt's Story

After more than 20 years in business, as a follower, employee, manager, leader, owner, and being the father of five great kids, it has become painfully obvious to me the parallels between managing and parenting. Rising into the management ranks at an early age, I was constantly asked by direct reports starting out their budding careers what they could do to gain the experience and practice necessary to advance up the corporate ranks so fast. I always told them the same thing: "You want practice and experience being a manager? Go have some kids." As I transitioned from employee to self-employed to business owner, I came to a hard realization when it came to being a father and husband.

When I was working on my doctoral dissertation[1], I decided to focus my study on employee burnout as it pertained to the construction industry. At the time, I was in the thick of it as a senior manager in the business. As I did preliminary research and fell upon burnout, I realized very quickly that I was burned out myself and it was obvious that the study was needed and might even help myself.

The entire study was conducted and written through the lens of an employee. Once I had transitioned beyond the employee space, past self-employed (solo-preneur), to business owner; I realized that employees worry about and seek work/life balance while entrepreneurs can't make this happen. There is no shutting it off when it comes to working in your passion. While employees can turn work off when they leave and worry about family during family time, entrepreneurs need to seek complete integration between work life and home life. There is no separation. The successful entrepreneur successfully integrates their family and work seamlessly. I spoke about this in greater detail in my best-selling book[2].

What I didn't talk about in the book though was the impact on the children because of this transition and integration. Integrating work and family for an entrepreneur is an ongoing, ever-changing, organic, dynamic thing. As soon as you make the effort to making it happen though, you can start to see immediate results in the strength and relationships that you hold most dear.

When I was an employee, my older kids Grayson, Logan, and Peighton saw me for about an hour in the evenings during the work-week. When Ella was a baby, she would go to bed around 6:00 pm each night, and I typically didn't get home from work until around 6:30-7:00. This meant that Monday through Friday I literally never got to spend any time with her.

As an entrepreneur, my schedule can be what I make it. I can be home and around so much more than I ever could be when I was working for someone else. As I spent more time with the kids, I could see an instant change in the relationships. My kids taught me the importance of integrating work and life.

We have gone on to create a lifestyle business that we can run from virtually anywhere we have an Internet connection and phone service (and we are working on eliminating the need for the phone). This has allowed us to take more trips, make more memories, and have amazing experiences together. It's this type of thing that reduces the stress and noise in life and puts you in a place to do more business. Funny how that works! You have more fun, you do more deals and have greater success!

My children used to tell me that they wanted to be an engineer or a nurse (like mommy or daddy). My kids wanted to know the names of our bosses at work and are interested in what you do and how things are going in our lives. It blew my young children's minds that I didn't have a boss. We sat and explained how mommy works at the hospital, and she has a boss, and that person has a boss, etc. But once we got all the way to the top of the organization chart, we explained that this is where daddy is at our company. The kids now talk about what business they want to start, what impact that they want to make, and how they can provide value to other kids and the world.

This makes me happy as a father and entrepreneur. My kids taught me the importance of integrating life and my passions on all levels. The more I work towards this goal, the more momentum it provides in our lives, and the more I want to work towards it.

## Grayson (age 10)

There were times that we would go to houses with dad and he would show us stuff and have us help him. A couple of things I learned from doing that was that it is hard work, but in the end, people pay us to live in these houses, so it is worth it. I also learned how to do a lot of different things. I think if we ever did some of those things again, I would know how to do them on my own. The last thing I learned was that no matter what I'm doing, my dad loves me and is there to help me if I need it.

## Logan (age 8)

I know what I learned! I learned to not work on houses without shoes on. I stepped on a nail, and it hurt really bad. Dad also taught us how to measure things and cut stuff. I learned the value of having skills. I like working on houses and doing the demo. I like kicking cabinet doors off! I think I want to work on houses when I grow up, like my dad.

## Peighton (age 6)

I like my daddy's office and that he doesn't have a boss. I get asked what I want to be when I grow up. I want to be a boss like my daddy or a nurse like mommy. I like that my dad is home more than he used to be when he had a boss.

## Ella (age 3)

I like that we get to do fun things like go on the Disney boat and go to the beach. I like that my daddy and mommy are home a lot to play with me.

[Matt: Having our own companies has provided us the opportunity to do things with the kids we were never able to do when we were working for someone else. The kids don't realize the difference, but they understand the experiences that we do together as a family.]

## Jaxson (age 1)

Jax isn't talking yet, but when I come into the room, he lights up and gets excited to see me. This is awesome when I think of his sister Ella who never saw me during the week. She didn't know who I was when she was his age. We have created a lifestyle and opportunity to actually know and connect with my kids on a much higher level.

# About Dr. Matt Motil

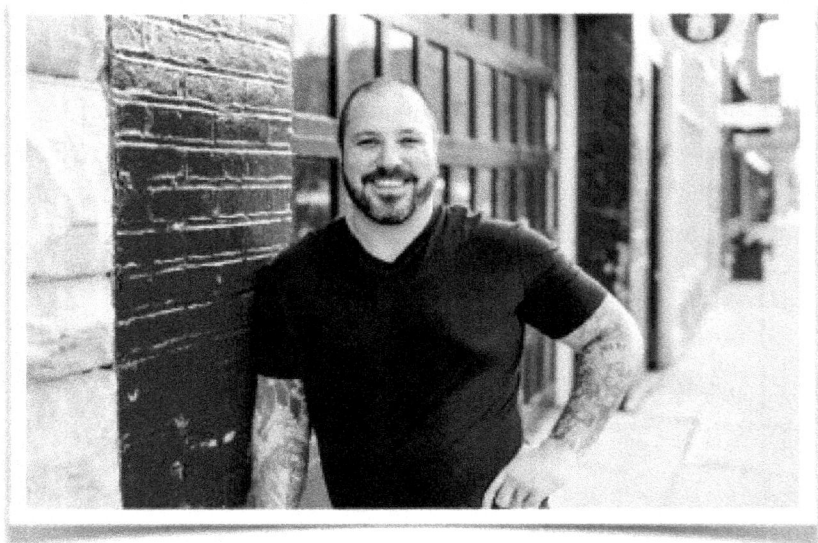

Dr. Matt Motil is a real estate entrepreneur, best-selling author, and host of the *Cashflow King Podcast*. He has worked with hundreds of investors from all over the world and helped them to grow massive wealth and passive income through remote real estate investments. After spending almost 20 years in the construction industry starting as a union laborer, working his way up to senior project management, he escaped the middle-class trap, utilizing rental real estate. Dr. Motil stopped teaching higher education when he realized he was simply helping people become better employees and now teaches people how to do exactly what he did, use real estate investing to fire their bosses forever!

Matt can be reached through his website

DrMattMotil.com

YouTube: DrMattMotil.tv

Instagram.com/DrMattMotil

Facebook.com/DrMattMotil

1: Project Duration, Budget, Individual Role, and Burnout Among Construction Managers. (2015).

2: Man on Fire: Lessons From a Perpetual Burnout on Creating Alignment for Success. (2017).
Get a FREE copy at ManOnFireBook.com

## Grayson, Logan, Peighton, Ella, and Jaxson Motil

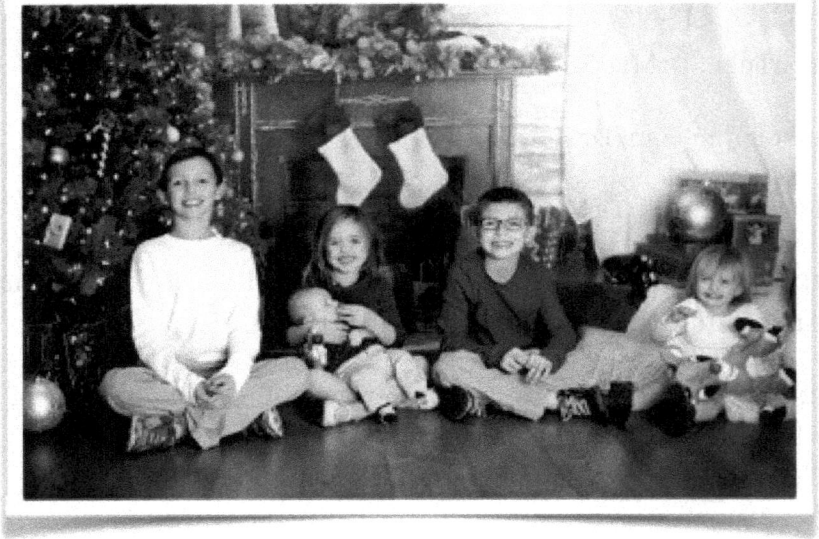

# Lessons That Last a Lifetime

## Jim's Story

I am the owner and manager of Habitation Investigation – a multi-inspector home inspection company servicing Columbus and all of Central Ohio. My wife Laura is the office manager, and we have client coordinators in the office to answer phones and do various tasks. With the staff and other systems that we have in place, realtors and clients can easily schedule home inspections, etc. Our company is steadily growing every year – nearly 35-40% every year for the past five years – and now I have some free time to spend with the family. Of course, I involve them whenever possible.

In business, the primary measurement of success is money. This is logical because without money the business cannot operate, and all businesses need cash flow to be able to pay employees. The lesson I learned from the kids was that money is not always the primary currency for everyone. I was later reminded of this by an adult client of ours.

Our company currently runs about as smoothly as it can, and with employees and systems, I'm able to take time to relax. The company did not originally operate that way. In the beginning, it was only myself in the business. I was doing the marketing, taking the phone calls while driving, answering questions about reports, scheduling inspections, building the website, and of course the inspections themselves.

While I was running and starting the business, I was also working nights in a factory. I worked in the factory from 11 PM till 7:30 AM, and then worked on the business during the days. I was surviving on only two to three hours of sleep each day for four or five days a week. I was feeling run down and on the verge of getting sick from being worn out all the time due to lack of sleep.

As I was getting ready to leave for work one night, my oldest child, Kaitlyn, ran up to me and asked me why I had to go to work. She was four or five years old at that time, and very cute of course. I said that I was going to work to earn money. To me, that was the logical and reasonable explanation. She says "Oh" in an excited manner, turned around and went into another room. I wondered where she was going and what she was doing, thinking maybe she was getting me something to take with me, or maybe that answer satisfied her. I was very wrong. She returned to me shortly, looking up at me while handing up to me play money. As she did this, she stated, "Here.....now you do not have to leave." She wanted to pay me to stay home.

She knew money had value and that could be used for all sorts of things. However, she was interested in time with me-not objects. This lesson has proven to be useful in regards to the company.

## The Lesson

When we do home inspections, the inspections are scheduled to start and end at specific times. We try to get there approximately

20 minutes early to avoid traffic or any issues with access codes to get into the home. One of our inspectors had a change in schedule and he started the inspection one hour earlier than the buyer had expected. When the home buyer arrived at the home and discovered he started earlier than scheduled, she was very upset. The inspector called the office to let us know about this, and I later heard about it over the phone from the buyer herself. After letting her vent a bit, I offered to go back out there to the home she was buying and spend as much time with her as she needed. That was all she wanted. She knew the inspector had already spent time and he did a complete inspection, what she really wanted was the time to be spent with her there.

As a result, all the inspectors are more conscious of being certain not to start an inspection too early. Each inspector tells the clients they are welcome to join us and follow us during the entire inspection if they wish. Most do not stay right next to the inspector all the time; however, the client knows they have that opportunity if they wish. Clients are also asked at the time of scheduling, and once again at the inspection, if they have any special concerns regarding the home. This makes them feel heard and special. As a result, we have many happy clients, and we have become one of the most reviewed home inspection companies in Ohio. Our past clients are happy and refer us to other home buyers.

## Kaitlyn's Story

My name is Kaitlyn Troth. I'm 16 years old now, but when I was a lot younger, my Dad worked the night shift at a factory. My Dad took the job out of necessity as my mother was about to lose her job. However, he had started a home inspection company a couple of years before, and he was now determined to make something of it.

So, Dad began working third shift at the factory during the night and during the day, worked to establish and develop his own company. Creating a company out of nothing is not an easy task under normal circumstances. Creating a company when you work third shift and get only two to three hours of sleep a day is even more difficult.

At this point, Habitation Investigation was a one-man show. Still in its early stages, Dad was the only person behind it. He did it all himself: the marketing, answering the phone calls, building the website, the scheduling, and the inspections themselves. As you can imagine, this was hard on him and he was always sleep deprived and on the brink of exhaustion. The company was making just enough to keep going.

Dad set a goal. He and my mother figured out what they needed for him to make at the company so he could work it full time. When he met that goal, he quit the factory and began working the company full time.

All his hard work paid off. He was able to quit the job he hated. Habitation Investigation is no longer a one-man show. He now has five inspectors in addition to himself and is currently training two more. There are now people that work in an actual office. Multiple systems are in place to keep everything running as smoothly as possible. The company is strong enough to support charities and covers a sizable area that is ever expanding. The company is also one of the most reviewed in the area on the Internet with an amazing reputation.

He has worked so hard to get the company where it's at today, and I'm so proud of him. He's one of the most ambitious and driven people I know, and he's taught me so much.

## The Lesson

You don't get anywhere by crossing your fingers and wishing for it. Dreams are very important, but you don't accomplish anything without working for it. If you want something, you need to be willing to work your ass off for it-procrastinating doesn't get you anywhere.

He's taught me all of this and more. And I'm forever grateful for it.

Thanks, Dad. I love you.

# About James M. Troth

Jim Troth is results-oriented professional with a broad range of experiences. He has a B.A. in Psychology and a minor in Philosophy from The Ohio State University. Jim's experiences include: supervisor, experience in the mental health field, sales, public speaking, martial artist, National Champion in Brazilian Jiu-jitsu (1999 and 2000 – a long time ago!), business owner/founder, and psychology research experience.

Jim is a highly-experienced home inspector whose company Habitation Investigation provides home inspection services throughout Columbus and Central Ohio. In addition to his home inspection services, Jim has been able to grow his company even during down times at rates to be admired. Habitation Investigation has grown into a multi-inspector company with the increased capacity to help home buyers and real estate professionals. Habitation Investigation offers the best warranties and has the highest reputation for excellence.

The website for the home inspection company is HomeInspectionsInOhio.com.

If you or a friend of yours is buying property in Central Ohio, be sure to contact them.

**Facebook**
Facebook.com/JimTroth

**LinkedIn**
LinkedIn.com/in/Jim-Troth-4686251

**Twitter**
Twitter.com/JimTroth

**Instagram**
Instagram.com/JimTroth

# About Kaitlyn A. Troth

Kaitlyn Troth, the daughter of Jim and Laura Troth, is sixteen years old and heading into her junior year of high school. She's an avid runner and runs cross country and track, even though she complains every time she runs.

She's taught herself to play the guitar, and while she's always working to improve on the guitar, she intends to learn more instruments. Right now, she's working on the drums! She loves music (Motionless in White and Marilyn Manson being among her favorites), as well as reading, writing, drawing, painting, and hanging out with her friends. She is an ardent fan of horror movies, and loves to binge watch Rupaul's Drag Race!

# What My Four Boys Taught ME About Business and LIFE!

## Andy's Stories

For over half of my life, I've been a dad.

As the father of four boys, there have been a ton of baseball games, wrestling, throwing balls in the house, heated arguments, a ton of laughter, and not a hint of pink in sight.

Over the course of 26+ years, I've probably learned more from my sons than they've ever learned from me.

I struggled to pick just one lesson that I learned from one of my boys, so instead, I've decided to pick something from each one of them that I felt may help you, as both a parent and as an entrepreneur, and just let 'er rip.

So here goes...

## Story #1: Making Courageous Decisions

The ups and downs of growing up lead to many highs and lows, not only for kids but also for their parents, especially when it's something you're dealing with for the first time.

My oldest son, Korbin, is the one whose first experiences are MY first experiences as a father.

Changing diapers, teaching how to ride a bike, making that first tackle, chipped teeth, watching them become parents, making mistakes, rewards and punishments... no one gives you an owner's manual when you become a parent.

Over the years, Korbin has probably been the most creative of all my boys, with a vivid imagination and great sense of humor.

At the same time, like most people, he's faced various challenges along the way that would make weaker men want to quit the game of life.

Not him, though.

While struggling with challenging circumstances around the age of 20, instead of throwing in the towel, he made a courageous decision - and then took action on it - by joining the U.S. Army.

I still remember him telling me, "Dad, this is what I need to do to get my life in order, so I'm doing it."

Three months later, my family and I were at Ft. Leonard Wood, Missouri attending his graduation from basic training, and I don't know that I've ever been more proud.

Not just for him graduating boot camp, but for facing his challenges head on through his commitment of sacrificing three plus years of his life to serve his country.

This spoke volumes for the type of character he has deep down inside.

We all make mistakes in our lives, but it's what we do to overcome those roadblocks that determine what kind of person we ultimately become.

He taught me, with that single decision, that I need to have the courage to make decisions in my business career that takes me out of my comfort zone so I can then enjoy the success I strive for.

## Story #2: Be Coachable and Implement What You Learn

My 2nd oldest son, Kurtis (more from him later), was probably the most coachable of my sons, as it relates to willingly listening to instruction and then implementing.

He and I have a strong connection through the game of baseball, among other things.

I remember when he was in kindergarten, he would always ask me if I'd take him out to a nearby field and let him hit some balls before his afternoon kindergarten class started.

From an early age, he would ask me questions about "How do you do this?" and as it relates to baseball, he would always do exactly what I taught him to do.

And then he'd practice, practice, practice.

The best kids to coach are those who are "coachable," willing to listen to instruction, and then IMPLEMENT what they're taught.

From all those years ago (he's now 23), I realized that I needed to be just as coachable in business, being willing to find a mentor who I trusted, listen closely to what I was taught, and then apply those fundamentals to my business.

## Story #3: Focus on One Thing Until It's Done

My youngest son, Kellen, has this amazing knack for being able to commit to a specific project and then putting the blinders on until it's done.

A couple of years ago, he got with a few friends in his third-grade class, and decided they were going to do a fundraising project for endangered animals.

He was the leader of this group and took it upon himself to take their ideas to the school's principal for permission to proceed.

Then for WEEKS, he tirelessly researched online, printed articles, downloaded images, and created a detailed report.

He also spearheaded the collection of money from those kids, parents, and school staff who agreed to contribute to this fundraising project, making around $1,000 in the process.

This was all done around his regular school studies, participating in sports, doing chores at home, and just having fun being a kid.

His 100% commitment and belief in this project led him to focus entirely on accomplishing his team's goals over the course of several weeks.

In turn, this was an example to me of how important it is to block out all distractions, and focusing entirely on the most important project at hand until it's ultimately completed.

## Story #4: Keeping the Faith Through Adversity

Our second oldest son, Kaden, began having seizures around his 1st birthday, and then struggled with those, off and on, for most of his childhood.

Through it all, though, between periods of having seizures or not (he's been seizure-free for 1.5 years now), Kaden taught ME a ton about perseverance and FAITH.

Before his brain surgery on March 8, 2012, when the surgeon explained to him, specifically, how they were about to cut his head open, his only concern was...

"Will I have a big screen TV in my room?"

This one little question sums up his overall attitude all these years that everything was going to be ok.

While I was second-guessing our decision to put Kaden through that surgery, almost to the point of tears, because of the fear I had inside, it was his faith (and my wife's assurances that we were doing the right thing) that kept me strong through all of that.

Looking back on that now, I realize how much he taught me that in life - as well as in business - you absolutely must have faith that everything is going to turn out well, as long as you have chosen a path that you believe is the best course of action for your particular situation.

## The Lesson

It took everyday real-world experiences with my kids to show me the light on how to properly approach my OWN life, but I also believe it can help you with your pursuits as an entrepreneur, as well, by remembering to...

1. Make courageous decisions.

2. Be coachable and implement what you learn.

3. Focusing on ONE project until it's done.

4. Keeping the faith through adversity.

Isn't it amazing what our kids can teach us, if we simply pay attention?

## Kurtis's Story – Expect to Win (And Always Hustle)

Before every baseball game from a young age, my dad, Andy, would always tell my teammates and I to "expect to win." A very simple quote that he pounded into the minds of every baseball team he has ever coached (he's still coaching my two younger brothers).

He not only preached "expect to win" in baseball, but he would also tell me to expect to win as I started out as an entrepreneur.

It's very important to have a winning mindset in everything you do. There are always going to be times of failure in life, and my dad has shown me that the people who build off their failure and simply keep going are the ones who succeed.

It's also important that you expect to win simply because not everyone is going to have your back.

When there aren't a lot a lot of people in your corner, and very few seem to support you, then you must have complete confidence in yourself if you ever want to succeed in business or in life, itself.

My dad had to deal with raising me when I wasn't always the most cooperative teenager, but one thing he simply would not tolerate was lack of hustle. When I was younger, I didn't quite understand the meaning of hustle. I understood hustle on the ballfield but didn't quite grasp why he was always preaching it to me in life.

After years of watching my dad become successful in business and life, through various ups and downs along the way, it all now makes sense.

Everything he does is 100% no excuses. Every minute of focused hustle is putting you ahead, and when it comes to your future those minutes add up.

I remember one time he was telling me the story about one of our games, years ago, that while he was coaching 3rd base, and we were down by five runs late in the game, that he thought we were beat.

Before you know it, our team came back to win that game, and he mentioned to me that HE (an adult) was reminded by US (a bunch of kids) that you never give up when the chips are down, and instead, always have faith that you're going to turn things around (expect to win).

Just by him pointing this out to me showed me that I'd already been living this "expect to win" attitude from an early age, and now that I have young kids of my own, I've chosen to live by this example, moving forward.

In fact, like my dad did before me, I've spent many hours learning the ropes of online marketing, "hustling" to find a path of success that's right for me, "expecting to win" every step of the way!

## The Lesson

This "expect to win" concept that I taught Kurtis, his brothers, and their teammates through 20 years of coaching youth baseball was about WAY more than just winning or losing ballgames.

Like I would tell them, not only will your positive expectations help you win more ballgames because of the confidence you have in yourself and each other, but this "expect to win" attitude will also help you in every area of your life.

As entrepreneurs, our lives are full of ups and downs, wins and losses, successes and failures.

You have to understand right from the start that it's not always going to be easy.

Once you're committed to achieving success in a particular business venture, you must have faith that you will reach your ultimate goals, no matter how tough things get (expect to win).

You also must persevere and keep pushing through the tough times (hustle?), knowing that as you overcome these obstacles, you'll be reminded of why you chose this entrepreneurial path to begin with.

To WIN!

And that you have what it takes to be successful in business, and in life, even if very few people believed in you along the way when you first got started (or even now, perhaps).

It's only through "expecting to win", and continuing to progress past the bumps in the road during your journey, that you'll be able to achieve the success that you've always known you are capable of.

# About Andy Hussong

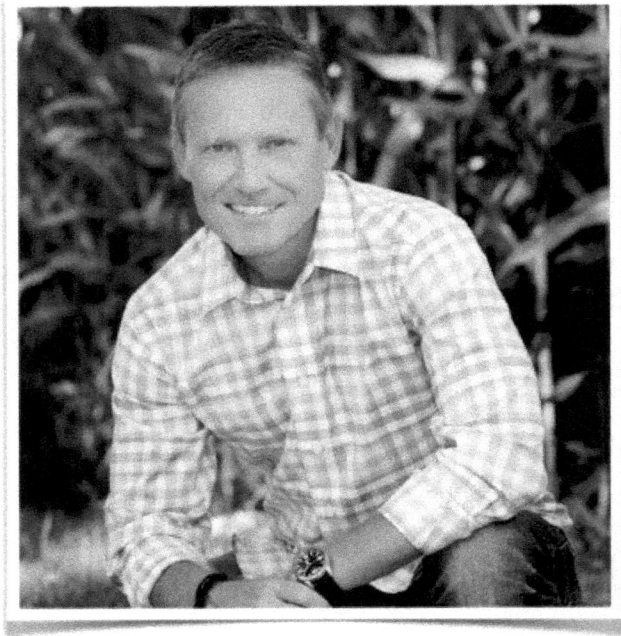

Andy Hussong is a highly-respected authority on the topics of online joint ventures and creating "endorsed influence" for his students and agency clients. Since 2005, he has been in-the-trenches, connecting and collaborating with hundreds of influencers, which has resulted in millions in profits for his clients. His proven systems help experts, authors, speakers, coaches, and consultants to expand their OWN influence by teaming up with other, like-minded influencers, resulting in joint venture deals that benefit all parties involved. Andy is also a devoted husband, father, grandfather, and longtime youth baseball coach from the heartland of America.

**Website**

EndorsedInfluence.com

**Facebook**

Facebook.com/AndyHussong

**LinkedIn**

LinkedIn.com/in/AndyHussong

## About Kurtis Hussong

Kurtis Hussong is a young entrepreneur and parent of two young children, committed to success, while he inspires others who are walking the same walk to achieve success on their terms. He is currently an apprentice and project manager at EndorsedInfluence.com, helping bring joint venture deals together, while also running various other ventures of his own.

**Facebook**

Facebook.com/Kurtis.Hussong

www.ingramcontent.com/pod-product-compliance
Lightning Source LLC
Chambersburg PA
CBHW060544200326
41521CB00007B/477